DK EYEWIT...

D0361593

15-MINUTE
LATIN-AMERICAN
SPANISH

DK EYEWITNESS TRAVEL

15-MINUTE
LATIN-AMERICAN
SPANISH

LEARN LATIN-
AMERICAN SPANISH
IN JUST 15
MINUTES A DAY

ANA BREMÓN

DK

London, New York, Munich, Melbourne, and Delhi

Dorling Kindersley Limited
Senior Editor Angeles Gavira
Project Art Editor Vanessa Marr
DTP Designer John Goldsmid
Production Controller Luca Frassinetti
Publishing Manager Liz Wheeler
Managing Art Editor Philip Ormerod
Publishing Director Jonathan Metcalf
Art Director Bryn Walls

Language content for Dorling Kindersley by
g-and-w publishing

Produced for Dorling Kindersley by
Schermuly Design Co.
Art Editor Hugh Schermuly
Project Editor Cathy Meeus
Special photography Mike Good

First American Edition, 2005
Published in the United States by
DK Publishing, Inc., 375 Hudson Street,
New York, New York 10014

05 06 07 08 09 10 9 8 7 6 5 4 3 2 1

A Cataloging-in-Publication record for this book
is available from the Library of Congress.

ISBN 0-7566-0925-9

15-Minute Latin-American Spanish is also
available in a pack with two CDs
ISBN 0-7566-0928-3

Color reproduction by Colourscan, Singapore
Printed and bound in China by Leo Paper
Products Limited

Contents

How to use this book

This main part of the book is devoted to 12 themed chapters, broken down into five 15-minute daily lessons, the last of which is a revision lesson. So, in just 12 weeks you will have completed the course. A concluding reference section contains a menu guide and English-to-Spanish and Spanish-to-English dictionaries.

Warm up and clock
Each day starts with a one-minute warm-up that encourages you to recall vocabulary or phrases you have learned previously. A clock to the right of the heading bar indicates the amount of time you are expected to spend on each exercise.

Instructions
Each exercise is numbered and introduced by instructions that explain what to do. In some cases additional information is given about the language point being covered.

Cultural/Conversational tip
These panels provide additional insights into life in Latin America and language usage.

Text styles
Distinctive text styles differentiate Spanish and English, and the pronunciation guide (see right).

In conversation
Illustrated dialogues reflecting how vocabulary and phrases are used in everyday situations appear throughout the book.

How to use the flap
The book's cover flaps allow you to conceal the Spanish so that you can test whether you have remembered correctly.

Revision pages
A recap of selected elements of previous lessons helps to reinforce your knowledge.

Useful phrases
Selected phrases relevant to the topic help you speak and understand.

Pronunciation guide

The Spanish of Latin America varies from country to country, although all are mutually comprehensible. This book teaches Mexican Spanish. A few sounds require special explanation:

c	a Spanish **c** is pronounced *s* before **i** or **e** but *k* before other vowels: **cinc** seenkoh (*five*)
h	is always silent: **hola** o-lah (*hello*)
j (g)	a Spanish **j** (and **g** before **i** or **e**) is pronounced as a strong *h*, as if saying <u>h</u>at emphasizing the first letter
ll	pronounced *y* as in <u>y</u>es
ñ	pronounced *ny* like the sound in the middle of *can<u>y</u>on*
r	a Spanish **r** is trilled like a Scottish **r**, especially at the beginning of a word and when doubled
v	a Spanish **v** is between an English *b* and *v*
z	a Spanish **z** is pronounced *s*

Spanish vowels tend to be pronounced shorter than their English equivalents:

a	as the English *f<u>a</u>ther*
e	as the English *w<u>e</u>t*
i	as the English *k<u>ee</u>p*
o	as the English *b<u>oa</u>t*
u	as the English *b<u>oo</u>t*

After each word or phrase you will find a pronunciation transcription, with underlining showing the stress. Remember that this can only be an approximation; there is no substitute for mimicking native speakers.

Say it
In these exercises you are asked to apply what you have learned using different vocabulary.

5 Say it

Do you have a single room, please?

For six nights.

Is breakfast included?

Dictionary
A mini-dictionary provides ready reference from English to Spanish and Spanish to English for 2,500 words.

Menu guide
Use this guide as a reference for food terminology and popular Latin American dishes.

132 DICTIONARY

Dictionary
English to Spanish

The gender of a Spanish noun is indicated by the word for *the* **el** and **la** (masculine and feminine singular) or their plural forms **los** (masculine) and **las** (feminine). Spanish adjectives (adj) vary according to the gender and number of the word they describe; the masculine form is shown here. In general, adjectives that end in "o" adopt an "a" ending in the feminine form, and those that end in "e" usually stay the same. For the plural, an "s" is added. Some words are used only in certain Latin American countries or regions, which are indicated by the following abbreviations:

126 MENU GUIDE

Menu guide

This guide lists the most common terms you may encounter on menus or when shopping for food. If you can't find an exact phrase, try looking up its component parts.

1 Warm up

The Warm Up appears at the beginning of each lesson. It will remind you of what you have already learned and prepare you for moving ahead with the new subject.

Hola
Hello

In Latin America it is common for women to greet each other with a kiss on the cheek. Men usually shake hands, although they may kiss or embrace younger male relatives or close friends. In formal situations— among strangers or in a business context—a handshake is the norm.

2 Words to remember

Look at these greetings and say them aloud. Conceal the text on the left with the cover flap and try to remember the Spanish for each item. Check your answers.

¡Hola!
o-lah
Hello!

Buenos días bwenos deeyas	*Good morning/day*
Me llamo Ana. may yamoh anna	*My name is Ana.*
Encantado/-a enkan-tadoh/-ah	*Pleased to meet you (male/female speaking)*
Buenas tardes (noches) bwenas tardes (noches)	*Good afternoon/ evening (night)*

Cultural tip Latin Americans frequently address people as "señor" (sir), "señora" (madam, for older women), and "señorita" (miss, for young women). With first names, use "Don" for men or "Doña" for women: Don Juan, Doña Ana.

3 In conversation: formal

Buenos días. Me llamo Concha García.
bwenos deeyas. may yamoh konchah garsee-ah

Good day. My name's Concha García.

José López, encantado.
hosay lopes, enkan-tadoh

José López, pleased to meet you.

Encantada.
enkan-tadah

Pleased to meet you.

4 Put into practice

Join in this conversation. Read the Spanish beside the pictures on the left and then follow the instructions to make your reply. Then test yourself by concealing the answers on the right with the cover flap.

Buenas tardes señor.
<u>bwe</u>nas <u>tar</u>des sen<u>yor</u>
Good evening, sir.

Say: Good evening, madam.

Buenas tardes señora.
<u>bwe</u>nas <u>tar</u>des sen<u>yor</u>ah

Me llamo Julia.
may <u>ya</u>moh <u>hool</u>ya
My name is Julia.

Say: Pleased to meet you.

Encantado.
enkan-<u>ta</u>doh

5 Useful phrases

Read these phrases aloud several times and try to memorize them. Conceal the Spanish with the cover flap and test yourself.

What's your name?	**¿Cómo se llama?** <u>ko</u>moh seh <u>ya</u>mah
Goodbye	**Adiós** addy-<u>os</u>
Thank you.	**Gracias.** <u>gra</u>syas
See you soon/ tomorrow.	**Hasta pronto/mañana.** <u>as</u>tah <u>pron</u>toh/ man<u>ya</u>nah

6 In conversation: informal

Entonces, ¿hasta mañana?
en<u>ton</u>ses, <u>as</u>tah man<u>ya</u>nah

So, see you tomorrow?

Sí, adiós.
see, addy-<u>os</u>

Yes, goodbye.

Adiós. Hasta pronto.
addy-<u>os</u>. <u>as</u>tah <u>pron</u>toh

Goodbye. See you soon.

Say "good morning" and "goodbye" in Spanish. (pp.8–9)

Now say "My name is…". (pp.8–9)

Say "sir" and "madam." (pp.8–9)

Las relaciones
Relatives

The Spanish equivalents of *mom* and *dad* are **mamá** and **papá**. The male plural can refer to both sexes—for example, **niños** (*boys* and *children*), **padres** (*fathers* and *parents*), **abuelos** (*grandfathers* and *grandparents*), **tíos** (*uncles* and *aunt and uncle*), **hermanos** (*brothers* and *siblings*), and so on.

2 Match and repeat

Look at the people in this scene and match their numbers with the list at the side. Read the Spanish words aloud. Now, conceal the list with the cover flap and test yourself.

1 **la hermana**
  lah airmanah

2 **el abuelo**
  el abweloh

3 **el padre**
  el pahdray

4 **el hermano**
  el airmanoh

5 **la abuela**
  lah abwelah

6 **la hija**
  lah ee-hah

7 **la madre**
  lah mahdray

8 **el hijo**
  el ee-hoh

❶ sister   ❷ grandfather   ❸ father   ❹ brother

❺ grandmother   ❻ daughter   ❼ mother   ❽ son

Conversational tip In Spanish, things as well as people are masculine or feminine—for example, "wine" is masculine: "*el* vino," but "milk" is feminine: "*la* leche." Use "los" and "las" for masculine and feminine plurals, respectively. For "a/an," use "un" for masculine and "una" for feminine items.

3 Words to remember: relatives

Familiarize yourself with these words. Read them aloud several
times and try to memorize them. Conceal the Spanish with the cover
flap and test yourself.

el marido **la esposa**
el mareedoh lah esposah
husband *wife*

Estoy casado/-a.
estoy ka<u>sa</u>doh/-ah
I'm married. (m/f)

father/mother-in-law	**el suegro/la suegra** el <u>swe</u>groh/lah <u>swe</u>grah
stepfather	**el padrastro** el pa<u>dras</u>-troh
stepmother	**la madrastra** lah ma<u>dras</u>-trah
children (male/female)	**los niños/las niñas** los <u>neen</u>yos/las <u>neen</u>yas
aunt/uncle	**la tía/el tío** lah <u>tee</u>-ah/el <u>tee</u>-oh
cousin	**el primo/la prima** el <u>pree</u>moh/lah <u>pree</u>mah
I have four children.	**Tengo cuatro niños.** <u>ten</u>goh <u>kwa</u>troh <u>neen</u>yos
I have two stepdaughters and a stepson.	**Tengo dos hijastras y un hijastro.** <u>ten</u>goh dos ee-<u>has</u>tras ee oon ee-<u>has</u>troh

4 Words to remember: numbers

Memorize these words and then test yourself using the cover flap.

Be careful when you
use the number one.
Used in front of a
word, **uno** changes to
un or **una**, depending
on whether the word
is masculine or
feminine. For
example: **Tengo un
hijo** (*I have one son*),
Tengo una hija (*I have
one daughter*).

one (m/f)	**uno/-a** <u>oo</u>noh/-ah
two	**dos** dos
three	**tres** tres
four	**cuatro** <u>kwa</u>troh
five	**cinco** <u>seen</u>koh
six	**seis** seys
seven	**siete** <u>sye</u>tay
eight	**ocho** <u>o</u>choh
nine	**nueve** <u>nwe</u>bay
ten	**diez** dee-<u>es</u>

5 Say it

I have five sons.

I have three sisters
and a brother.

I have two children.

1 Warm up

Say the Spanish for as many members of the family as you can. (pp.10–11)

Say "I have two sons." (pp.10–11)

Mi familia
My family

There are two ways of saying *you* in Spanish, **usted** for formal situations and **tú** in informal ones. There is also a formal way of saying *your*—**su** (singular) and **sus** (plural): **usted y su esposa** (*you and your wife*), **¿Son ésos sus hijos?** (*Are those your sons?*). **Su** and **sus** also mean *his* and *her*.

2 Words to remember

Say these words out loud a few times. Conceal the Spanish with the cover flap and try to remember the Spanish word for each item.

mi *mee*	*my (with singular)*
mis *mees*	*my (with plural)*
tu *too*	*your (informal, with singular)*
tus *toos*	*your (informal, with plural)*
su *soo*	*your (formal, with singular)*
sus *soos*	*your (formal, with plural)*
su *soo*	*his/her (with singular) their (with singular)*
sus *soos*	*his/her (with plural) their (with plural)*

Éstos son mis padres.
<u>es</u>tos son mees <u>pah</u>dres
These are my parents.

3 In conversation

¿Tiene usted niños?
<u>tye</u>nay oos<u>ted</u> <u>neen</u>yos

Do you have any children?

Sí, tengo dos hijas.
see, <u>ten</u>goh dos <u>ee</u>-has

Yes, I have two daughters.

Éstas son mis hijas. ¿Y usted?
<u>es</u>tas son mees <u>ee</u>-has. ee oos<u>ted</u>

These are my daughters. And you?

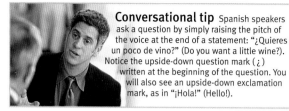

Conversational tip Spanish speakers ask a question by simply raising the pitch of the voice at the end of a statement: "¿Quieres un poco de vino?" (Do you want a little wine?). Notice the upside-down question mark (¿) written at the beginning of the question. You will also see an upside-down exclamation mark, as in "¡Hola!" (Hello!).

4 Useful phrases

Read these phrases aloud several times and try to memorize them. Conceal the Spanish with the cover flap and test yourself.

Do you have any brothers? (formal)	**¿Tiene usted hermanos?** <u>tye</u>nay oo<u>sted</u> air<u>ma</u>nos
Do you have any brothers? (informal)	**¿Tienes hermanos?** <u>tye</u>nes air<u>ma</u>nos

This is my husband.	**Éste es mi marido.** <u>es</u>tay es mee ma<u>ree</u>doh
That's my wife.	**Ésa es mi esposa.** <u>e</u>sah es mee es<u>po</u>sah

Is that your sister? (formal)	**¿Ésa es su hermana?** <u>e</u>sah es soo air<u>ma</u>nah
Is that your sister? (informal)	**¿Ésa es tu hermana?** <u>e</u>sah es too air<u>ma</u>nah

No, pero tengo un hijastro. noh, <u>pe</u>roh <u>ten</u>goh oon ee-<u>has</u>troh

No, but I have a stepson.

5 Say it

Do you have any brothers and sisters? (formal)

Do you have any children? (informal)

I have two sisters.

This is my wife, María.

1 Warm up

Say "See you soon." (pp.8–9)

Say "I am married" (pp.10–11) and "I have a wife." (pp.12–13)

Ser y tener
To be and to have

Two of the most important verbs are **ser** (*to be*) and **tener** (*to have*). Note that there are different ways of saying *you, we,* and *they,* with formal and informal, singular and plural, and masculine and feminine forms. Pronouns (*I, you,* etc.) are omitted where the sense is clear.

2 Ser: to be

Familiarize yourself with **ser** (*to be*). When you are confident, practice the sample sentences below. Note: there is another verb meaning "to be"—**estar**, which is discussed on page 49.

yo soy yoh soy	*I am*
tú eres too <u>eh</u>-res	*you are (informal singular)*
usted es oos<u>ted</u> es	*you are (formal singular)*
él es el es	*he is*
ella es <u>eh</u>-yah es	*she is*
nosotros/-as somos no<u>sotros</u>/-as <u>somos</u>	*we (male/female) are*
ustedes son oos<u>tedes</u> son	*you are (plural)*
ellos/ellas son <u>eh</u>-yos/<u>eh</u>-yas son	*they (male/female) are*

Yo soy inglesa.
yoh soy eeng<u>lesah</u>
I'm English.

¿De dónde es usted? day <u>don</u>day es oos<u>ted</u>	*Where are you from?*
Es mi hermana. es mee air<u>man</u>ah	*She is my sister.*
Somos mexicanos. <u>s</u>omos mehee<u>kan</u>os	*We're Mexican.*

3 Tener: to have

Practice **tener** (*to have*) and the sample sentences, then test yourself.

I have	**yo tengo** yoh <u>ten</u>goh
you have *(informal singular)*	**tú tienes** too <u>tye</u>nes
you have *(formal singular)*	**usted tiene** oo<u>sted</u> <u>tye</u>nay
he has	**el tiene** el <u>tye</u>nay
she has	**ella tiene** <u>eh</u>-yah <u>tye</u>nay
we (male/female) *have*	**nosotros/-as tenemos** no<u>so</u>tros/-as te<u>nay</u>mos
you have *(plural)*	**ustedes tienen** oos<u>ted</u>es <u>tye</u>nen
they (male/female) *have*	**ellos/ellas tienen** <u>eh</u>-yos/<u>eh</u>-yas <u>tye</u>nen

¿Tiene rosas rojas?
<u>tye</u>nay <u>ro</u>sas <u>rro</u>has
Do you have red roses?

He has a meeting.	**Tiene una reunión.** <u>tye</u>nay <u>oo</u>nah reh-oon<u>yon</u>
Do you have a *cell phone?*	**¿Tiene usted celular?** <u>tye</u>nay oos<u>ted</u> seloo<u>lar</u>
How many brothers *and sisters do you* *have?*	**¿Cuantos hermanos** **tiene usted?** <u>kwan</u>tos air<u>ma</u>nos <u>tye</u>nay oos<u>ted</u>

4 Negatives

It is easy to make sentences negative in Spanish—just put **no** in front of the verb: **No somos ingleses** (We're not English).

la bicicleta
lah beesee<u>kle</u>tah
bicycle

I'm not Spanish.	**No soy español.** noh soy espan<u>yol</u>
He's not vegetarian.	**No es vegetariano.** noh es be-hetar<u>ya</u>noh
We don't have any *children.*	**No tenemos niños.** noh te<u>nay</u>mos <u>nee</u>nyos

No tengo coche.
noh <u>ten</u>goh <u>ko</u>chay
I don't have a car.

Respuestas
Answers
Cover with flap

Repase y repita
Review and repeat

1 How many?

1 tres
tres

2 nueve
nwebay

3 cuatro
kwatroh

4 dos
dos

5 ocho
ochoh

6 diez
dee-es

7 cinco
seenkoh

8 siete
syetay

9 seis
seys

2 Hello

1 **Buenos días. Me llamo... [your name].**
bwenos deeyas. may yamoh...

2 **Encantado/-a.**
enkan-tadoh/-ah

3 **Sí, y tengo dos hijos. ¿Y usted?**
see, ee tengoh dos ee-hos. ee oosted

4 **Adiós. Hasta mañana.**
addy-os. astah manyanah

1 How many?

Hide the answers with the cover flap. Then say these Spanish numbers aloud. Check to see if you remembered the Spanish correctly.

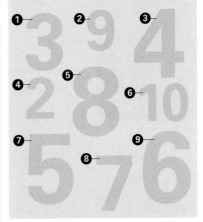

2 Hello

You are talking to someone you have just met. Join in the conversation, replying in Spanish following the English prompts.

Buenos días. Me llamo María.
1 *Answer the greeting and give your name.*

Éste es mi marido, Juan.
2 *Say "Pleased to meet you."*

¿Está usted casado/-a?
3 *Say "Yes, and I have two sons. And you?"*

Nosotros tenemos tres hijos.
4 *Say "Goodbye. See you tomorrow."*

3 To have or be

Fill in the blanks with the correct form of **tener** (*to have*) or **ser** (*to be*). Check to see if you remembered the Spanish correctly.

1 Yo _____ inglesa.

2 Nosotros _____ cuatro niños.

3 Yo no _____ feliz.

4 ¿Tú _____ coche?

5 Él _____ mi marido.

6 Yo no _____ teléfono móvil.

7 Tú no _____ español.

8 ¿ _____ usted hijos?

3 To have or be

1 **soy**
   soy

2 **tenemos**
   te<u>nay</u>mos

3 **soy**
   soy

4 **tienes**
   t<u>ye</u>nes

5 **es**
   es

6 **tengo**
   <u>tengoh</u>

7 **eres**
   <u>eh</u>-res

8 **Tiene**
   t<u>ye</u>nay

4 Family

Say the Spanish for each of the numbered family members. Check to see if you remembered the Spanish correctly.

❷ *grandfather*

sister ❶   ❸ *father*

❹ *brother*

❻ *daughter*   ❽ *son*

❺ *grandmother*   ❼ *mother*

4 Family

1 **la hermana**
   lah air<u>man</u>ah

2 **el abuelo**
   el ab<u>wel</u>oh

3 **el padre**
   el <u>pah</u>dray

4 **el hermano**
   el air<u>man</u>oh

5 **la abuela**
   lah ab<u>wel</u>ah

6 **la hija**
   lah <u>ee</u>-hah

7 **la madre**
   lah <u>mah</u>dray

8 **el hijo**
   el <u>ee</u>-hoh

Warm up

Count to ten.
(pp.10–11)

Say "hello" and
"goodbye." (pp.8–9)

Ask "Do you have a
son?" (pp.14–15)

En la cafetería
At the café

Throughout Latin America you will
find **las cafeterías**, small cafés that also
serve alcohol. You can often get bread,
toast, or pastries with your coffee in
the mornings. In Mexico these are
collectively known as **pan dulce**.
Churros (fried dough sticks) are also a
popular snack, originating in Spain.

Words to remember

Familiarize yourself with these words.

el chocolate
el chokolatay
hot chocolate

el té con limón el tay kon lee<u>mon</u>	*tea with lemon*
el café descafeinado el ka<u>fay</u> deskafey<u>na</u>doh	*decaffeinated coffee*
el café americano el ka<u>fay</u> ameree<u>ka</u>noh	*large, weak black coffee*
la mermelada lah mermel<u>a</u>dah	*jam*
el pan tostado con mantequilla el pan tos<u>ta</u>doh kon mante<u>kee</u>-yah	*toast with butter*

el café negro
el ka<u>fay</u> <u>ne</u>groh
black coffee

Cultural tip Look for traditional strong black coffee such
as "café chico" in Argentina or the Mexican cinnamon-flavored
"café de olla." If you want tea with milk, ask for "té con leche."
If you just ask for "té," you are likely to get black tea.

In conversation

**Buenos días. Me da
un café con leche.**
<u>bwe</u>nos <u>dee</u>yas. may
dah oon ka<u>fay</u> kon
<u>le</u>chay

*Hello. I'll have coffee
with milk.*

¿Eso es todo?
<u>e</u>soh es <u>to</u>doh

Is that all?

¿Tiene churros?
<u>tye</u>nay <u>choo</u>rros

*Do you have any
churros?*

4 Useful phrases

Practice these phrases. Read the English under the pictures and say the phrase in Spanish as shown on the right. Then use the cover flap to test yourself.

los churros
los choorros
churros

el azúcar
el ah-sookar
sugar

Me da un café negro.
may dah oon kafay negroh

I'll have black coffee.

¿Eso es todo?
esoh es todoh

Is that all?

Yo voy a tomar churros.
yoh boy ah tomar choorros

I'm going to have some churros.

el café con leche
el kafay kon lechay
coffee with milk

¿Cuánto es?
kwantoh es

How much is that?

Sí, señor.
see, senyor

Yes, sir.

Gracias. ¿Cuánto es?
grasyas. kwantoh es

Thank you. How much is that?

Veinte pesos, por favor.
beyntay paysos, por fabor

Twenty pesos, please.

Ask "How much is that?" (pp.18–19)

Say "I don't have a brother." (pp.14–15)

Ask "Do you have any churros?" (pp.18–19)

En el restaurante
In the restaurant

There is a huge variety of eating places in Latin America, from the largely male-dominated working-class **cantinas** to five-star **restaurantes** and **haciendas**. Inns serving traditional food are variously known as **fondas** and **posadas**, and you can also often get snacks in cafés and bars.

Words to remember

Memorize these words. Conceal the Spanish with the cover flap and test yourself.

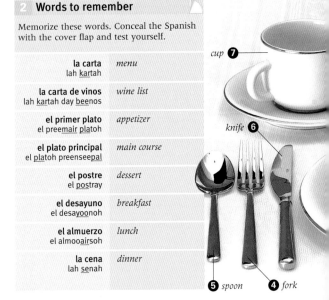

la carta lah <u>kar</u>tah	*menu*
la carta de vinos lah <u>kar</u>tah day <u>bee</u>nos	*wine list*
el primer plato el pree<u>mair</u> <u>plat</u>oh	*appetizer*
el plato principal el <u>plat</u>oh preen<u>see</u>pal	*main course*
el postre el <u>pos</u>tray	*dessert*
el desayuno el desa<u>yoo</u>noh	*breakfast*
el almuerzo el almoo<u>air</u>soh	*lunch*
la cena lah <u>se</u>nah	*dinner*

cup **7**

knife **6**

5 *spoon* **4** *fork*

In conversation

Hola. Una mesa para cuatro, por favor.
<u>o</u>-lah. <u>oo</u>nah <u>me</u>sah <u>pa</u>rah <u>kwa</u>troh, por fa<u>bor</u>

Hello. A table for four, please.

¿Tiene una reservación?
<u>tye</u>nay <u>oo</u>nah resair<u>ba</u>syon

Do you have a reservation?

Sí, a nombre de Cortés.
see, ah <u>nom</u>bray day kor<u>tes</u>

Yes, in the name of Cortés.

4 Match and repeat

Look at the numbered items in this table setting and match them with the vocabulary list at the side. Read the Spanish words aloud. Then conceal the list with the cover flap and test yourself.

glass **1**

8 *saucer*

napkin **2**

plate **3**

1 **la copa**
  lah <u>ko</u>pah

2 **la servilleta**
  lah serbee-<u>ye</u>tah

3 **el plato**
  el <u>pla</u>toh

4 **el tenedor**
  el tene<u>dor</u>

5 **la cuchara**
  lah koo<u>cha</u>rah

6 **el cuchillo**
  el koo<u>chee</u>-yoh

7 **la taza**
  lah <u>ta</u>sah

8 **el platito**
  el pla<u>tee</u>toh

5 Useful phrases

Practice these phrases and then test yourself using the cover flap to conceal the Spanish.

What do you have for dessert?	**¿Qué tiene de postre?** kay <u>tye</u>nay day <u>pos</u>tray
The check, please.	**La cuenta, por favor.** lah <u>kwen</u>tah, por fa<u>bor</u>

¿Fumadores o no fumadores?
fooma<u>do</u>res oh noh fooma<u>do</u>res

Smoking or nonsmoking?

No fumadores, por favor.
noh fooma<u>do</u>res, por fa<u>bor</u>

Nonsmoking, please.

Síganme, por favor.
<u>see</u>gan-may, por fa<u>bor</u>

Follow me, please.

Querer
To want

Querer (*to want*) is a verb that is essential to everyday conversation. There is also a polite form, **quisiera** (*I'd like*). Use this when requesting something because **quiero** (*I want*) may sound too strong: ¿Qué quiere beber? (*What do you want to drink?*); **Quisiera un café** (*I'd like coffee*).

2 Querer: to want

Say the different forms of **querer** (*to want*) aloud. Use the cover flaps to test yourself and, when you are confident, practice the sample sentences below.

yo quiero yoh kyairoh	*I want*
tú quieres/usted quiere too kyaires/oosted kyairay	*you want (singular informal/formal)*
él/ella quiere e/eh-yahl kyairay	*he/she wants*
nosotros/-as queremos nosotros-as keraymos	*we want (masculine/feminine)*
ustedes quieren oostedes kyairen	*you want (plural)*
ellos/ellas quieren eh-yos/eh-yas kyairen	*they (male/female) want*
¿Quieres vino? kyaires beenoh?	*Do you want some wine?*
Quiere un coche nuevo. kyairay oon kochay nweboh	*She wants a new car.*

Quiero dulces.
kyairoh doolses
I want some candy.

Conversational tip In general, Latin Americans are polite and formal, using "gracias" and "por favor" continuously and addressing each other as "señor/señora" and "don/doña." You may also hear people say "con permiso" when passing you in a crowded place. You should reply "pase usted" as you stand aside to let them through.

③ Polite requests

There is a form of **quiero** (*I want*) used for polite requests: **quisiera** (*I'd like*). Practice these sample phrases.

I'd like a beer.

Quisiera una cerveza.
keesyairah oonah
sairvaysah

I'd like a table for tonight, please.

Quisiera una mesa para esta noche, por favor.
keesyairah oonah
mesah parah estah
nochay, por fabor

I'd like to see the menu, please.

Quisiera ver la carta, por favor.
keesyairah ber lah
kartah, por fabor

④ Put into practice

Join in this conversation. Read the Spanish beside the pictures on the left and follow the instructions to make your reply. Then test yourself by concealing the answers with the cover flap.

Buenas tardes señor. ¿Tiene una reservación?
bwenas tardes senyor.
tyeneh oonah
resairbasyon
Good evening, sir. Do you have a reservation?

Say: No, but I would like a table for three.

No, pero quisiera una mesa para tres.
noh, peroh keesyairah
oonah mesah parah
tres

Muy bien. ¿Qué mesa le gustaría?
mwee byen. kay mesah
le goostareeyah
Fine. Which table would you like?

Say: Near the window, please.

Cerca de la ventana, por favor.
serkah day lah
bentanah, por fabor

Warm up

Say "She's happy" and "I'm not sure." (pp.14–15)

Ask "Do you have churros?" (pp.18–19)

Say "I'd like coffee with milk." (pp.18–19)

Los platos
Dishes

Latin America offers a large variety of regional dishes. Common elements are corn and chili, but local specialties include steak from Argentina, Mexican spicy **mole** chocolate sauce, and Peruvian raw-fish **ceviche**. The cuisine is largely meat- or fish-based, and vegetarians should ask for advice.

Cultural tip At lunch time, you will find that many restaurants offer "el menú del día" (the day's set menu). This is usually a three-course meal with bread and a drink included in the price.

Match and repeat

Match the numbered items to the Spanish words in the panel.

1 **las verduras**
las berdooras

2 **la fruta**
lah frootah

3 **el queso**
el kesoh

4 **los frutos secos**
los frootos sekos

5 **la sopa**
lah sopah

6 **las aves**
las ahbes

7 **el pescado**
el peskadoh

8 **la pasta**
lah pastah

9 **el marisco**
el mareeskoh

10 **la carne**
lah karnay

❶ vegetables

❷ fruit

❸ cheese

❺ soup

❻ poultry

❽ pasta

❾ seafood

3 Words to remember: cooking methods

The ending often varies depending on the gender of item described.

fried (m/f)	**frito/-a** freetoh/-ah
grilled	**a la plancha** ah lah planchah
roasted (m/f)	**asado/-a** ahsadoh/-ah
boiled (m/f)	**hervido/-a** erbeedoh/-ah
steamed	**al vapor** al bapor
rare (m/f)	**poco cocido/-a** pokoh koseedoh/-ah

Quisiera mi filete bien cocido.
keesyairah mee feeletay byen koseedoh
I'd like my steak well done.

6 Say it

What is a "tortilla"?

I'm allergic to seafood.

I'd like a beer.

4 Words to remember: drinks

Familiarize yourself with these words.

water	**el agua** el ahgwah
sparkling water	**el agua con gas** el ahgwah kon gas
still water	**el agua sin gas** el ahgwah seen gas
wine	**el vino** el beenoh
beer	**la cerveza** lah sairbaysah
fruit juice	**el jugo** el hoogoh

4 *nuts*

7 *fish*

5 Useful phrases

Learn these phrases and then test yourself.

I'm a vegetarian.	**Soy vegetariano/-a.** soy be-hetaryanoh/-ah
I am allergic to nuts.	**Soy alérgico/-a a los frutos secos.** soy alerheekoh/ah a los frootos sekos
What is "conejo"?	**¿Qué es "conejo"?** kay es kone-hoh

10 *meat*

Repase y repita
Review and repeat

At the table

1 **los frutos secos**
los <u>froo</u>tos <u>se</u>kos

2 **el marisco**
el ma<u>ree</u>skoh

3 **la carne**
lah <u>kar</u>nay

4 **el azúcar**
el ah-<u>soo</u>kar

5 **la copa**
lah <u>ko</u>pah

At the table

Name the numbered items.

1 nuts
2 seafood
3 meat
4 sugar
5 glass

This is my...

1 **Ésta es mi esposa.**
<u>es</u>tah es mee es<u>po</u>sah

2 **Éstas son sus hijas.**
<u>es</u>tas son soos <u>ee</u>-has

3 **Su mesa es de no fumadores.**
soo <u>me</u>sah es day noh fooma<u>do</u>res

This is my...

Say these phrases in Spanish.
Use **mi(-s)**, **tu(-us)**, or **su(-s)**.

1 *This is my wife.*

2 *These are her daughters.*

3 *Their table is non-smoking.*

I'd like...

1 **Quisiera un café negro.**
kee<u>sya</u>irah oon <u>ka</u>fay <u>ne</u>groh

2 **Quisiera churros.**
kee<u>sya</u>irah <u>choo</u>rros

2 **Quisiera azúcar.**
kee<u>sya</u>irah ah-<u>soo</u>kar

4 **Quisiera un café con leche.**
kee<u>sya</u>irah oon <u>ka</u>fay kon <u>le</u>chay

I'd like...

Say "I'd like" the following:

1 black coffee
2 churros
3 sugar
4 coffee with milk

6 *pasta*

knife **7**

8 *cheese*

beer **10**

9 *napkin*

At the table

6 **la pasta**
  lah pastah

7 **el cuchillo**
  el koochee-yoh

8 **el queso**
  el kesoh

9 **la servilleta**
  lah serbee-yetah

10 **la cerveza**
   lah sairbaysah

Restaurant

You arrive at a restaurant. Join in the conversation, replying in Spanish following the English prompts.

Buenas tardes señora, señor.
1 *Say: I'd like a table for six.*

¿Fumadores o no fumadores?
2 *Say: Nonsmoking.*

Síganme, por favor.
3 *Ask for the menu.*

¿Quiere la carta de vinos?
4 *Say: No. Sparkling water, please.*

Muy bien.
5 *Say: I don't have a glass.*

Restaurant

1 **Quisiera una mesa para seis.**
  bwenas tardes, keesyairah oonah mesah parah seys

2 **No fumadores.**
  noh foomadores

3 **La carta, por favor.**
  lah kartah, por fabor

4 **No. Agua con gas, por favor.**
  noh. ahgwah kon gas, por fabor

5 **No tengo copa.**
  noh tengoh kopah

1 Warm up

Say "he is" and "they are." (pp.14–15)

Say "he is not" and "they are not." (pp.14–15)

What is Spanish for "the children"? (pp.10–11)

Los días y los meses
Days and months

In Spanish, days of the week (**los días de la semana**) and months (**los meses**) do not have capital letters. Notice that you use **en** with months: **en abril** (*in April*), but **el** or **los** with days: **el/los lunes** (*on Monday/Mondays*).

2 Words to remember: days of the week

Familiarize yourself with these words and test yourself using the flap.

lunes loones	*Monday*
martes martes	*Tuesday*
miércoles myairkoles	*Wednesday*
jueves hwebes	*Thursday*
viernes byernes	*Friday*
sábado sabadoh	*Saturday*
domingo domeengoh	*Sunday*
hoy oy	*today*
mañana manyanah	*tomorrow*
ayer ah-yair	*yesterday*

Nos reunimos mañana.
nos reh-ooneemos manyanah
We meet tomorrow.

Tengo una reservación para hoy.
tengoh oonah resairbasyon parah oy
I have a reservation for today.

3 Useful phrases: days

Practice these phrases and then test yourself using the cover flap.

La reunión no es el martes. lah reh-oonyon noh es el martes	*The meeting isn't on Tuesday.*
Trabajo los domingos. traba-hoh los domeengos	*I work on Sundays.*

4 Words to remember: months

Familiarize yourself with these words and test yourself using the flap.

Nuestro aniversario es en julio.
nwestroh
aneebairsaree-oh es en
hoolee-oh
Our anniversary is in July.

La Navidad es en diciembre.
lah nabeedad es en deesyembray
Christmas is in December.

January	**enero**	ehneroh
February	**febrero**	febreroh
March	**marzo**	marsoh
April	**abril**	abreel
May	**mayo**	mah-yoh
June	**junio**	hoonee-oh
July	**julio**	hoolee-oh
August	**agosto**	agostoh
September	**septiembre**	septyembray
October	**octubre**	oktoobray
November	**noviembre**	nobyembray
December	**diciembre**	deesyembray
month	**el mes**	el mes
year	**el año**	el anyoh

5 Useful phrases: months

Practice these phrases and then test yourself using the cover flap.

My children are on vacation in August.	**Mis hijos están de vacaciones en agosto.** mees ee-hos estan day bakasyones en agostoh
My birthday is in June.	**Mi cumpleaños es en junio.** mee koomplay-anyos es en hoonee-oh

1 Warm up

Count in Spanish from 1 to 10. (pp.10–11)

Say "I have a reservation." (pp.20–1)

Say "The meeting is on Wednesday." (pp.28–9)

La hora y los números
Time and numbers

The hour is preceded by **la** as in **la una** (*one o'clock*) and **las** for other numbers: **las dos**, **las tres**, and so on. In English, minutes sometimes come first: *ten to five*; in Spanish, the hour comes first: **las cinco menos diez** (*"five minus ten"*).

2 Words to remember: time

Memorize how to tell the time in Spanish.

la una lah <u>oo</u>nah	*one o'clock*
la una y cinco lah <u>oo</u>nah ee <u>seen</u>koh	*five after one*
la una y cuarto lah <u>oo</u>nah ee <u>kwar</u>toh	*quarter after one*
la una y media lah <u>oo</u>nah ee <u>medee</u>-ah	*one-thirty*
la una y veinte lah <u>oo</u>nah ee <u>beyn</u>tay	*one-twenty*
las dos menos cuarto las dos <u>men</u>os <u>kwar</u>toh	*quarter to two*
las dos menos diez las dos <u>men</u>os dee-<u>es</u>	*ten to two*

3 Useful phrases

Practice these phrases and then test yourself using the cover flap.

¿Qué hora es? kay <u>orah</u> es	*What time is it?*
¿A qué hora quiere el desayuno? ah kay <u>orah</u> <u>kyairay</u> el desah-<u>yoo</u>noh	*What time do you want breakfast?*
La reunión es a mediodía. lah reh-<u>oon</u>yon es ah maydyo<u>dee</u>-ah	*The meeting is at noon.*

4 Words to remember: higher numbers

To say 21 you use **veinti** and add **uno** (*one*): **veintiuno**. Successive numbers are created in the same way—for example, **veintidós** (22), **veintitrés** (23), and so on. After 30, link the numbers with **y** (*and*): **treinta y uno** (31), **cuarenta y cinco** (45), **sesenta y seis** (66).

Note the special forms used for 500, 700, and 900: **quinientos**, **setecientos**, and **novecientos**.

Quiero el autobús cincuenta y tres.
<u>kyai</u>roh el a<u>oo</u>to<u>boos</u>
seenk<u>wen</u>tah ee tres
I want the Route 53 bus.

eleven	**once**	<u>on</u>say
twelve	**doce**	<u>do</u>say
thirteen	**trece**	<u>tre</u>say
fourteen	**catorce**	ka<u>tor</u>say
fifteen	**quince**	<u>keen</u>say
sixteen	**dieciséis**	deeayseesa<u>yees</u>
seventeen	**diecisiete**	deeayseeseeaytay
eighteen	**dieciocho**	deeays<u>yo</u>choh
nineteen	**diecinueve**	deeaysyn<u>we</u>bay
twenty	**veinte**	<u>beyn</u>tay
thirty	**treinta**	<u>treyn</u>tah
forty	**cuarenta**	kwa<u>ren</u>tah
fifty	**cincuenta**	seenk<u>wen</u>tah
sixty	**sesenta**	se<u>sen</u>tah
seventy	**setenta**	se<u>ten</u>tah
eighty	**ochenta**	o<u>chen</u>tah
ninety	**noventa**	no<u>ben</u>tah
one hundred	**cien**	<u>see</u>ayn
two hundred	**doscientos**	dos-<u>seeayn</u>tos
five hundred	**quinientos**	keenee<u>ayn</u>tos
one thousand	**mil**	meel
two thousand	**dos mil**	dos meel
one million	**un millón**	oon mee-<u>yon</u>

5 Say it

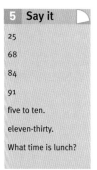

25

68

84

91

five to ten.

eleven-thirty.

What time is lunch?

1 Warm up

Say the days of the week. (pp.28–9)

Say "three o'clock." (pp.30–1)

What's the Spanish for "today," "tomorrow," and "yesterday"? (pp.28–9)

Las citas
Appointments

Business in Latin America is generally conducted more formally than in the United States. People also tend to leave the office for the lunch hour, often having a sit-down meal. Remember to use the formal forms of "you" (**usted**, **ustedes**) in business situations.

2 Useful phrases

Learn these phrases and then test yourself.

¿Nos reunimos mañana? nos reh-oo<u>nee</u>mos man<u>ya</u>nah	*Shall we meet tomorrow?*
¿Con quién? kon kee-<u>en</u>	*With whom?*
¿Cuándo estás libre? <u>kwan</u>doh es<u>tas</u> <u>lee</u>bray	*When are you free?*
Lo siento, estoy ocupado/-a. loh <u>syen</u>toh, es<u>toy</u> okoo<u>pa</u>doh/-ah	*I'm sorry, I'm busy. (male/female)*
¿Qué tal el jueves? keh tal el <u>hwe</u>bes	*How about Thursday?*
Para mí está bien. <u>pa</u>rah mee es<u>tah</u> byen	*That's good for me.*

el apretón de manos
el apre<u>ton</u>
day <u>ma</u>nos
handshake

Bienvenido.
byenve<u>nee</u>doh
Welcome.

3 In conversation

Buenos días. Tengo una cita.
<u>bwe</u>nos <u>dee</u>yas. <u>ten</u>goh <u>oo</u>nah <u>see</u>tah

Good morning. I have an appointment.

¿Con quién es la cita?
kon kee-<u>en</u> es lah <u>see</u>tah

With whom is the appointment?

Con el Señor Montoya.
kon el sen<u>yor</u> mon<u>to</u>yah

With Mr. Montoya.

4 Put into practice

Join in this conversation. Read the Spanish beside the pictures on the left and then follow the instructions to make your reply. Then test yourself by concealing the answers on the right with the cover flap.

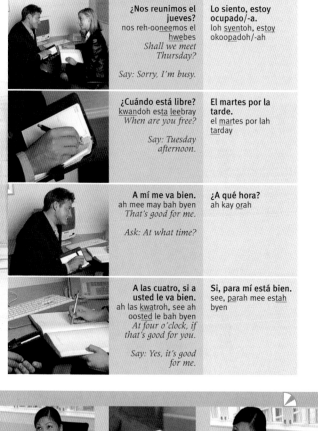

¿Nos reunimos el jueves?
nos reh-ooneemos el hwebes
Shall we meet Thursday?

Say: Sorry, I'm busy.

Lo siento, estoy ocupado/-a.
loh syentoh, estoy okoopadoh/-ah

¿Cuándo está libre?
kwandoh esta leebray
When are you free?

Say: Tuesday afternoon.

El martes por la tarde.
el martes por lah tarday

A mí me va bien.
ah mee may bah byen
That's good for me.

Ask: At what time?

¿A qué hora?
ah kay orah

A las cuatro, si a usted le va bien.
ah las kwatroh, see ah oosted le bah byen
At four o'clock, if that's good for you.

Say: Yes, it's good for me.

Sí, para mí está bien.
see, parah mee estah byen

Muy bien. ¿A qué hora?
mwee byen. ah kay orah

Fine. What time?

A las tres, pero llego un poco tarde.
ah las tres, peroh yegoh oon pokoh tarday

At three o'clock, but I'm a little late.

No se preocupe. Tome asiento, por favor.
noh say pre-ohkoopay. tomay asyaintoh, por fabor

Don't worry. Take a seat, please.

1 Warm up

Say "I'm sorry."
(pp.32–3)

What is the Spanish
for "I'd like an
appointment"?
(pp.32–3)

How do you say
"when?" in Spanish?
(pp.32–3)

Por teléfono
On the telephone

There are many telephone centers
throughout Latin America where you
can call overseas for flat rates. Phone
cards—available from newsstands,
grocers, and other small shops—can
be used with public phones, although
international lines may be erratic.

2 Match and repeat

Match the numbered items to the Spanish
in the panel on the left, then test yourself.

1 **el cargador**
el kargador

2 **el contestador
automático**
el kontestador
aootomateekoh

3 **la tarjeta
telefónica**
lah tarhetah
telefoneekah

4 **el celular**
el seloolar

5 **los auriculares**
los aooreekoolares

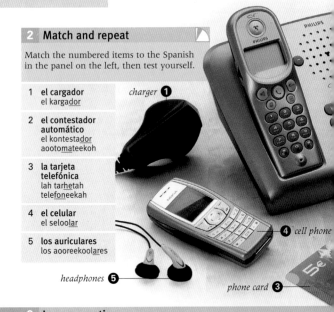

charger ❶

❹ *cell phone*

headphones ❺

phone card ❸

3 In conversation

**Dígame, habla con
Susana Castillo.**
deegamay, ablah kon
soosanah kasteeyoh

*Hello. Susana Castillo
speaking.*

**Buenos días. Quisiera
hablar con Julián
López, por favor.**
bwenos deeyas.
keesyairah hablar kon
hooleean lopes, por
fabor

*Hello. I'd like to speak
to Julián López, please.*

¿De parte de quién?
day partay day kee-en

Who's calling?

4 Useful phrases

Learn these phrases. Then test yourself using the cover flap.

I'd like an outside line.

Quisiera una línea externa.
keesyairah oonah leeneah externah

Quisiera llamar por cobrar.
keesyairah yamar por kobrar
I'd like to make a collect call.

I'd like to speak to María Alfaro.

Quisiera hablar con María Alfaro.
keesyairah ablar kon mareeah alfaroh

2 answering machine

Can I leave a message?

¿Puedo dejar un mensaje?
pwedoh dehar oon mensahay

5 Say it

I'd like to speak to Mr. Girona.

Can I leave a message for Antonio?

Sorry, I have the wrong number.

Perdone, me equivoqué de número.
perdonay, may ekeebokay day noomeroh

José Ortega, de Imprentas Lacuesta.
hosay ortegah, day eemprentas lakwestah

José Ortega of Lacuesta Printers.

Lo siento. La línea está ocupada.
loh syaintoh. lah leeneah estah okoopadah

I'm sorry. The line is busy.

¿Le puede decir que me llame, por favor?
lay pweday deseer kay may yamay, por fabor

Can you ask him to call me, please?

Repase y repita
Review and repeat

1 Sums

1 **dieciséis**
deeayseesayees

2 **treinta y nueve**
treyntah ee
nwebay

3 **cincuenta y tres**
seenkwentah ee
tres

4 **setenta y cuatro**
setentah ee
kwatroh

5 **noventa y nueve**
nobentah ee
nwebay

1 Sums

Say the answers to these sums out loud in Spanish. Then check to see if you remembered correctly.

1 $10 + 6 = ?$

2 $14 + 25 = ?$

3 $66 - 13 = ?$

4 $40 + 34 = ?$

5 $90 + 9 = ?$

3 Telephones

What are the numbered items in Spanish?

cell phone ❶

phone card ❸

2 To want

1 **Quiere**
kyairay

2 **quiere**
kyairay

3 **queremos**
keraymos

4 **quieres**
kyaires

5 **quiero**
kyairoh

6 **quieren**
kyairen

2 To want

Fill in the blanks with the correct form of **querer** (*to want*).

1 ¿ _____ usted un café?

2 Ella _____ ir de vacaciones.

3 Nosotros _____ una mesa para tres.

4 Tú _____ una cerveza.

5 Yo _____ caramelos.

6 Ellos _____ una mesa para dos.

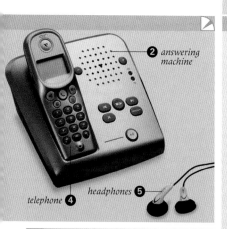

answering machine **2**

telephone **4**

headphones **5**

3 Telephones

1 **el celular**
el seloolar

2 **el contestador automático**
el kontestador
aootomateekoh

3 **la tarjeta telefónica**
lah tarhetah
telefoneekah

4 **el teléfono**
el telefonoh

5 **los auriculares**
los aooreekoolares

4 When?

What do these sentences mean?

1 **Tengo una cita el lunes veinte de mayo.**

2 **Mi cumpleaños es en septiembre.**

3 **Hoy es domingo.**

4 **No trabajo por las tardes.**

4 When?

1 *I have a meeting on Monday, May 20th.*

2 *My birthday is in September.*

3 *Today is Sunday.*

4 *I don't work in the afternoons.*

5 Time

Say these times in Spanish.

5 Time

1 **la una**
lah oonah

2 **la una y cinco**
las oonah ee
seenkoh

3 **la una y veinte**
lah oonah ee
beyntay

4 **la una y media**
lah oonah ee
medee-ah

5 **la una y cuarto**
lah oonah ee
kwartoh

6 **las dos menos diez**
las dos menos
dyes

1 Warm up

Count to 100 in tens.
(pp.10–11, pp.30–1)

Ask "What time is it?"
(pp.30–1)

Say "One-thirty."
(pp.30–1)

En la taquilla
At the ticket office

The once widespread rail network in Latin America is now in decline, replaced by a system of long-distance buses. However, you can still make journeys by train along classic routes such as the Panama Railroad beside the Panama Canal or the dramatic Copper Canyon Railway in Mexico.

2 Words to remember

Learn these words and then test yourself.

la estación lah estas<u>yon</u>	*(train) station*
la central lah sen<u>tral</u>	*(bus) station*
el boleto el bo<u>lay</u>toh	*ticket*
de ida day <u>ee</u>dah	*one-way*
de ida y vuelta day <u>ee</u>dah ee <u>bwel</u>tah	*round-trip*
de primera de pree<u>mer</u>ah	*first class*
de segunda day se<u>goon</u>dah	*second class*
el descuento el des<u>kwen</u>toh	*discount*

el pasajero
el pasa<u>hair</u>oh
passenger

la señal
lah sen<u>yal</u>
sign

La estación está llena de gente.
lah estas<u>yon</u> es<u>tah</u> <u>yen</u>ah day <u>hen</u>tay
The station is crowded.

3 In conversation

Dos boletos para Veracruz, por favor.
dos bo<u>lay</u>tos <u>par</u>ah bera<u>kroos</u>, por fa<u>bor</u>

Two tickets to Veracruz, please.

¿De ida y vuelta?
day <u>ee</u>dah ee <u>bwel</u>tah

Round-trip?

Sí. ¿Necesito reservar asiento?
see. nese<u>see</u>toh rreseer<u>bar</u> asy<u>ain</u>toh

Yes. Do I need to reserve seats?

4 Useful phrases

Practice these phrases and then test yourself using the cover flap.

How much is a ticket to Veracruz?
¿Cuánto cuesta un boleto para Veracruz?
kwantoh kwaystah oon bolaytoh parah berakroos

Can I pay by credit card?
¿Puedo pagar con tarjeta de crédito?
pwedoh pagar kon tarhetah de kredeetoh

Mi tren va con retraso.
mee tren bah kon rretrasoh
My train is late.

Do I have to change trains?
¿Tengo que cambiar?
tengoh kay kambee-ar

el tren | **el andén**
el tren | el anden
train | *platform*

Which platform does the train leave from?
¿De qué andén sale el tren?
day kay anden salay el tren

Are there any discounts?
¿Hay algún descuento?
ah-ee algoon deskwentoh

What time does the train to Tampico leave?
¿A qué hora sale el tren para Tampico?
ah kay orah salay el tren parah tampeekoh

5 Say it

Which platform does the train to Cusco leave from?

Three return tickets to Monterrey, please.

Cultural tip
Buying seats for tourist trains can usually be done either at the station or through tour agencies.

No hace falta. Noventa pesos, por favor.
noh ahsay faltah. nobentah paysos, por fabor
That's not necessary. Ninety pesos, please.

¿Aceptan tarjetas de crédito?
ahseptan tarhetas day kredeetoh
Do you take credit cards?

Sí. El tren sale del andén cinco.
see. el tren salay del anden seenkoh
Yes. The train leaves from platform five.

1 Warm up

What is "train" in Spanish? (pp.38–9)

What does "¿De qué andén sale el tren?" mean? (pp.38–9)

Ask "When are you free?" (pp.32–3)

Ir y tomar
To go and to take

The verbs **ir** (*to go*) and **tomar** (*to take*) allow you to create many useful sentences. Note that **tomar** can also mean *to drink*: **tomar café** (*to drink coffee*). If no drink is specified then alcohol is implied: **yo nunca tomo** (*I never drink alcohol*). It can also mean *to turn*: **tomar a la derecha** (*to turn right*).

2 Ir: to go

Spanish uses the same form of **ir** for both *I go* and *I am going*: **voy a México** (*I am going to Mexico/I go to Mexico*). The same is true of other verbs—for example, **tomo el metro** (*I am taking the metro/I take the metro*).

yo voy yoh boy	*I go*
tú vas/usted va too bas/oos<u>ted</u> bah	*you go (informal/ formal singular)*
él/ella va el/<u>eh</u>-yah bah	*he/she goes*
nosotros/-as vamos no<u>so</u>tros/-as <u>ba</u>mos	*we go*
ustedes van oos<u>te</u>des ban	*you go (plural)*
ellos/ellas van <u>eh</u>-yos/<u>eh</u>-yas ban	*they go*
¿A dónde vas? ah <u>don</u>day bas	*Where are you going?*
Voy a Perú. boy ah pai<u>roo</u>	*I am going to Peru.*

Voy al centro.
boy al <u>sen</u>troh
I am going downtown.

Conversational tip You may have noticed that "de" (of) combines with "el" to produce "del" as in "el menú del día" (menu of the day). In the same way, "a" (to) combines with "el" to produce "al": "Voy al museo" (I'm going to the museum). With feminine and plural words "de" remains separate from "la," "los," and "las": "los días de la semana" (days of the week).

3 Tomar: to take

Say the present tense of **tomar** (*to take*) aloud. Use the flaps to test yourself and, when you are confident, practice the sentences below.

yo tomo yoh <u>to</u>moh	*I take*
tú tomas/usted toma too <u>to</u>mas/oos<u>ted</u> <u>to</u>mah	*you take (informal/ formal singular)*
él toma el <u>to</u>mah	*he takes*
ella toma <u>eh</u>-yah <u>to</u>mah	*she takes*
nosotros/-as tomamos no<u>so</u>tros/-as to<u>ma</u>mos	*we take*
ustedes toman oos<u>te</u>des toman	*you take (plural)*
ellos/ellas toman <u>eh</u>-yos/<u>eh</u>-yas toman	*they take*

Yo tomo el metro todos los días.
yoh <u>to</u>moh el <u>me</u>troh <u>to</u>dos los <u>dee</u>yas
I take the metro every day.

No quiero tomar un taxi. noh <u>kyai</u>roh tomar oon <u>tak</u>see	*I don't want to take a taxi.*
Tome la primera a la izquierda. <u>to</u>may lah pree<u>me</u>rah ah lah ees<u>kyai</u>rdah	*Take the first left.*

4 Put into practice

Cover the text on the right and complete the dialogue in Spanish.

¿A dónde va? ah <u>don</u>day bah *Where are you going?* Say: *I'm going to the museum.*	**Voy al museo.** boy al moo<u>say</u>oh
¿Quiere tomar el autobús? <u>kyai</u>ray tomar el aoo<u>to</u>boos *Do you want to take the bus?* Say: *No, I want to go by metro.*	**No, quiero ir en metro.** noh, <u>kyai</u>roh eer en <u>me</u>troh

1 Warm up

Say "I don't want to take a taxi."
(pp.40–1)

Ask "Where are you going?" (pp.40–1)

Say "80" and "40."
(pp.30–1)

Taxi, autobús, y metro
Taxi, bus, and metro

The word for "bus" varies throughout the Spanish-speaking world. In southern Latin America it is **ómnibus**, in Mexico **camión**, in other parts of Central America it is **gua-gua**, while in the rest of Latin America it is **autobús**.

2 Words to remember

Familiarize yourself with these words.

el autobús el aootoboos	*bus*
la taquilla lah takeeyah	*ticket office*
la estación de metro lah estasyon day metroh	*metro station*
la parada de autobús lah paradah day aootoboos	*bus stop*
la tarifa lah tareefah	*fare*
el taxi el taksee	*taxi*
la parada de taxis lah paradah day taksees	*taxi stand*

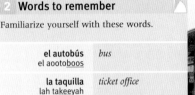

¿Para aquí el 17?
parah ahkee el deeayseeseeaytay
Does the Route 17 bus stop here?

3 In conversation: taxi

Al Parque España, por favor.
al parkay espanyah, por fabor

To España Park, please.

Sí, de acuerdo, señor.
see, day akwairdo, senyor

Yes, certainly, sir.

¿Me puede dejar aquí, por favor?
may pweday dehar ahkee, por fabor

Can you drop me here, please?

4 Useful phrases

Practice these phrases and then test yourself using the cover flap.

I'd like a taxi to go to the Congress.	**Quisiera un taxi para ir al Congreso.** keesyairah oon taksee parah eer al kongraysoh
When is the next bus?	**¿Cuándo sale el próximo autobús?** kwandoh salay el prokseemoh aootoboos
How do you get to the cathedral?	**¿Cómo se va a la catedral?** komoh say bah ah lah katedral
How long is the trip?	**¿Cuánto dura el viaje?** kwantoh doorah el beeahay
Please wait for me.	**Espéreme, por favor.** esperemay, por fabor

Cultural tip Although the main forms of urban transport are buses and taxis, several capital cities, including Mexico City, Santiago, and Buenos Aires, do have efficient and fast underground metro systems.

6 Say it

Do you go near the train station?

Do you go near the cathedral?

When's the next bus to Morelia?

5 In conversation: bus

¿Pasa cerca del museo? pasah serkah del moosayoh

Do you go near the museum?

Sí. Son 80 centavos. see. son ochentah sentavos

Yes. That's 80 centavos.

Avíseme cuando lleguemos. abeesemay kwandoh yeghemos

Tell me when we arrive.

1 Warm up

How do you say "I have..."? (pp.14–15)

Say "my father," "my sister," and "my parents." (pp.12–13)

Say "I'm going to Santiago." (pp.40–1)

En la carretera
On the road

Expressways (**autopistas**) are generally good in the more developed areas of Latin America, although a toll (**cuota**) is often charged. Other roads can be unpaved, poorly maintained, and often have inadequate signage, so extra care should be taken, especially when driving at night.

2 Match and repeat

Match the numbered items to the list on the left, then test yourself.

1 **la cajuela**
lah kahwelah

2 **el parabrisas**
el parabreesas

3 **el cofre**
el kofray

4 **la rueda**
lah rwedah

5 **la llanta**
lah yantah

6 **la puerta**
lah pwertah

7 **el parachoques**
el parachokes

8 **los faros**
los faros

Cultural tip It is customary to give a tip to the gas station attendant, who will check your oil and tires and clean your windshield on request.

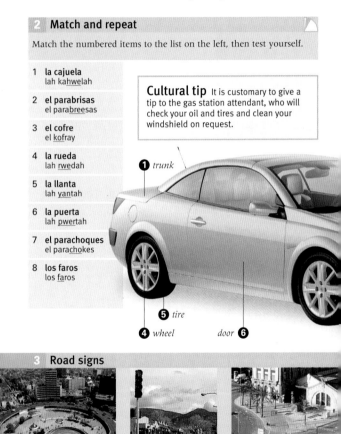

❶ trunk

❺ tire

❹ wheel door ❻

3 Road signs

la glorieta
lah gloryetah

roundabout

el semáforo
el semaforoh

traffic lights

el cruce
el kroosay

intersection

4 Useful phrases

Learn these phrases and then test yourself using the cover flap.

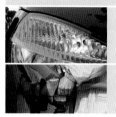

The turn signal doesn't work.

La direccional no funciona.
lah deereksyonal noh foonsyonah

Fill it up, please.

Lleno, por favor.
yennoh, por fabor

5 Words to remember

Familiarize yourself with these words, then test yourself using the flap.

6 Say it

There's something wrong with my engine.

I have a flat tire.

2 *windshield*

3 *hood*

7 *bumper*   *headlights* **8**

gasoline	**la gasolina** lah gasoleenah
diesel	**el diesel** el deesel
oil	**el aceite** el ah-sayeetay
engine	**el motor** el motor
gearbox	**la caja de cambios** lah kahah day kambyos
turn signal	**la direccional** lah deereksyonal
flat tire	**la llanta ponchada** lah yantah ponchadah
exhaust	**el tubo de escape** el tooboh day eskapay
driver's license	**la licencia de manejar** lah leesensyah day manehar

la autopista
lah aootopeestah

expressway/highway

la autopista de peaje
lah aootopeestah day pyahay

toll expressway

el embotellamiento
el embotellamyentoh

traffic jam

Respuestas
Answers
Cover with flap

Repase y repita
Review and repeat

1 Transportation

1 **el autobús**
el aootoboos

2 **el taxi**
el taksee

3 **el coche**
el kochay

4 **la bicicleta**
lah beeseekletah

5 **el metro**
el metroh

1 Transportation

Name these forms of transportation in Spanish.

bus **1**

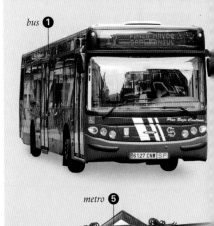

metro **5**

2 Go and take

1 **ir**
eer

2 **tomo**
tomoh

3 **va**
bah

4 **vamos**
bamos

5 **toman**
toman

6 **voy**
boy

2 Go and take

Use the correct form of the verb in brackets.

1 Quiero ____ a la estación. (ir)

2 Yo ____ el metro. (tomar)

3 ¿A dónde ____ usted? (ir)

4 Nosotros ____ al centro. (ir)

5 Ellos ____ un taxi.
(tomar)

6 Yo ____ a México.
(ir)

Respuestas
Answers
Cover with flap

2 taxi

3 car

4 bicycle

You?

Use the correct formal or informal form of the verb in each sentence.

1 *You are in a café. Ask "Do you have churros?"*

2 *You are with a friend. Ask "Do you want a beer?"*

3 *A visitor approaches you at your company reception. Ask "Do you have an appointment?"*

4 *You are on the bus. Ask "Do you go near the station?"*

5 *Ask your mother where she's going tomorrow.*

You?

1 **¿Tiene churros?**
tyenay choorros

2 **¿Quieres una cerveza?**
kyaires oonah sairbaysah

3 **¿Tiene una cita?**
tyenay oonah seetah

4 **¿Pasa cerca de la estación?**
pasah serkah day lah estasyon

5 **¿A dónde vas mañana?**
ah donday bas manyanah

Tickets

You're buying tickets at a train station. Follow the conversation, replying in Spanish following the numbered English prompts.

¿Qué desea?
1 *I'd like two tickets to Morelia.*

¿De ida o de ida y vuelta?
2 *Round-trip, please.*

Muy bien. Ochenta pesos, por favor.
3 *What time does the train leave?*

A las tres y diez.
4 *What platform does the train leave from?*

Andén número siete.
5 *Thank you very much. Goodbye.*

Tickets

1 **Quisiera dos boletos para Morelia.**
keesyairah dos bolaytos parah moraylyah

2 **De ida y vuelta, por favor.**
day eedah ee bweltah, por fabor

3 **¿A qué hora sale el tren?**
ah kay orah salay el tren

4 **¿De qué andén sale el tren?**
day kay anden salay el tren

5 **Muchas gracias. Adiós.**
moochas grasyas. addy-os

1 Warm up

Ask "How do you get to the museum?" (pp.42–3)

Say "I want to take the metro" and "I don't want to take a taxi" (pp.40–1)

En la ciudad
Around town

Note that the Spanish word **museo** (*museum*) also means art gallery when it's a public building in which works of art are exhibited; **galería de arte** usually refers to a shop that sells works of art. Be careful, too, not to confuse **librería** (*bookshop* or *bookshelf*) and **biblioteca** (*library*).

2 Match and repeat

Match the numbered locations to the words in the panel.

1 **el ayuntamiento**
el ahyoonta-<u>myain</u>toh

2 **el puente**
el <u>pwen</u>tay

3 **el centro**
el <u>sen</u>troh

4 **la iglesia**
lah ee<u>gle</u>seeah

5 **la plaza**
lah <u>pla</u>sah

6 **el estacionamiento**
el estasyona-<u>myain</u>toh

7 **la biblioteca**
lah bibleeoh<u>te</u>kah

8 **el museo**
el moo<u>say</u>oh

❶ town hall

❷ bridge

church ❹

downtown ❸

❺ *square*

❼ *library*

3 Words to remember

Familiarize yourself with these words and test yourself using the cover flap.

la gasolinera la gasoleе<u>ne</u>rah	*gas station*
la oficina de información turística lah ohfee<u>see</u>nah day eenformas<u>yon</u> tooree<u>stee</u>kah	*tourist information*
la piscina municipal lah pees<u>see</u>nah mooneesee<u>pal</u>	*public swimming pool*

Conversational tip In Spanish there are two ways of saying "am," "is," or "are." You have already learned the verb "ser" (p.14): "soy inglés" (I am English); "es vegetariano" (he is vegetarian). When talking about where something is, you need to use a different verb: "estar." The most important forms of this verb are: "estoy" (I am), "está" (he/she/it is), and "están" (they are): "¿Dónde está la iglesia?" (Where is the church?); "El cafetería no está lejos." (The café isn't far.)

4 Useful phrases

Practice these phrases and then test yourself using the cover flap.

La catedral está en el centro.
lah katedral estah en el sentroh
The cathedral is downtown.

Is there an art gallery in town?	**¿Hay algún museo de arte en la ciudad?** ah-ee algoon moosayoh day artay en lah syoodad
Is it far from here?	**¿Está lejos de aquí?** estah lehos day ahkee
There is a swimming pool near the bridge.	**Hay una piscina cerca del puente.** ah-ee oonah peesseenah serkah del pwentay

5 Put into practice

Join in this conversation. Read the Spanish on the left and follow the instructions to make your reply. Then test yourself.

¿Le puedo ayudar? lay pwedoh ahyoodar *Can I help you?* *Ask: Is there a library in town?*	**¿Hay alguna biblioteca en la ciudad?** ah-ee algoonah bibleeohtekah en lah syoodad
No, pero hay un museo. noh, peroh ah-ee oon moosayoh *No, but there's a museum.* *Ask: How do I get to the museum?*	**¿Cómo se va al museo?** komoh say bah al moosayoh
Está por allí. estah por ahyee *It's over there.* *Say: Thank you very much.*	**Muchas gracias.** moochas grasyas

6 *parking lot*

8 *museum*

Las direcciones
Directions

1 Warm up

How do you say "near the station"? (pp.42–3)

Say "Take the first left." (pp.40–1)

Ask "Where are you going?" (pp.40–1)

You'll often be able to find a **mapo de la ciudad** (*town map*) in the downtown area, usually near the town hall or tourist office. In the older parts of Latin American towns there are often narrow streets, in which you will usually find a one-way system in operation. Parking is usually restricted.

el bloque de oficinas
el blokay day ohfeeseenas
office block

2 Useful phrases

Learn these phrases and then test yourself.

Dé vuelta a la izquierda/derecha. day vweltah ah lah eeskyairdah/ derechah	*Turn left/right.*
todo recto todoh rrektoh	*straight ahead*
¿Cómo se va a la piscina? komoh say bah ah lah peesseenah	*How do I get to the swimming pool?*
la primera a la derecha lah preemerah ah lah derechah	*first right*
la segunda a la izquierda lah segoondah ah lah eeskyairdah	*second left*

la fuente
lah fwentay
fountain

3 In conversation

¿Hay un restaurante aquí cerca?
ah-ee oon restaoorantay ahkee serkah

Is there a restaurant nearby?

Sí, cerca de la estación.
see, serkah day lah estasyon

Yes, near the station.

¿Cómo se va a la estación?
komoh say bah ah lah estasyon

How do I get to the station?

4 Words to remember

Familiarize yourself with these words and test yourself using the flap.

Me perdí.
may perdee
I'm lost.

el centro deportivo
el sentroh deporteeboh
gym

**la zona
peatonal**
lah sonah
pe-ahtonal
pedestrian zone

traffic lights	**el semáforo** el semaforoh
corner	**la esquina** lah eskeenah
street/road	**la calle** lah kayay
main road	**la calle principal** lah kayay preenseepal
at the end of the street	**al final de la calle** al feenal day lah kayay
map	**el mapa** el mapah
overpass	**el paso elevado** el pasoh elebadoh
across from	**enfrente de** enfrentay day

¿Dónde estamos?
donday estamos
Where are we?

5 Say it

Turn right at the end of the street.

Turn left across from the museum.

It's ten minutes by bus.

Dé vuelta a la izquierda en el semáforo.
day vweltah ah lah eeskyairdah en el semaforoh

Turn left at the traffic lights.

¿Está lejos?
estah lehos

Is it far?

No, cinco minutos andando.
noh, seenkoh meenootos andandoh

No, it's five minutes on foot.

1 Warm up

Say the days of the week in Spanish. (pp.28–9)

How do you say "six o'clock"? (pp.30–1)

Ask "What time is it?" (pp.30–1)

El turismo
Sightseeing

Many national museums and art galleries close on Mondays. Although stores are normally closed on Sundays, many will open in tourist areas. In provincial areas, it is not unusual for public buildings and shops to close at lunchtime, between 2:00 and 4:00 pm.

2 Words to remember

Familiarize yourself with these words and test yourself using the flap.

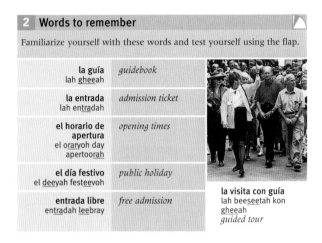

la guía lah <u>ghee</u>ah	*guidebook*
la entrada lah en<u>tra</u>dah	*admission ticket*
el horario de apertura el o<u>rar</u>yoh day aper<u>too</u>rah	*opening times*
el día festivo el <u>dee</u>yah fes<u>tee</u>voh	*public holiday*
entrada libre en<u>tra</u>dah <u>lee</u>bray	*free admission*

la visita con guía
lah bee<u>see</u>tah kon <u>ghee</u>ah
guided tour

Cultural tip If a public holiday falls on a Thursday or a Tuesday, people will often "hacer puente" (do a bridge)—in other words, take Friday or Monday off to make a long weekend.

3 In conversation

¿Abren esta tarde?
<u>ah</u>bren es<u>tah tar</u>day

Are you open this afternoon?

Sí, pero cerramos a las cuatro.
see, <u>pe</u>roh ser<u>ra</u>mos ah las <u>kwa</u>troh

Yes, but we close at four o'clock.

¿Tienen acceso para sillas de ruedas?
<u>tye</u>nen ak<u>se</u>soh <u>pa</u>rah <u>see</u>yas day <u>rwe</u>das

Do you have access for wheelchairs?

4 Useful phrases

Practice these phrases and then test yourself using the cover flap.

What time do you open/close?

¿A qué hora abre/cierra?
ah kay orah ahbray/syairrah

Where are the restrooms?

¿Dónde están los baños?
donday estan los banyos

Is there access for wheelchairs?

¿Hay acceso para sillas de ruedas?
ah-ee aksesoh parah seeyas day rwedas

5 Put into practice

Cover the text on the right and complete the dialogue in Spanish.

Lo siento, el museo está cerrado.
loh syentoh, el moosayoh estah serradoh
Sorry. The museum is closed.

Ask: Are you open on Tuesdays?

¿Abren los martes?
ahbren los martes

Sí, pero cerramos temprano.
see, peroh serramos tempranoh
Yes, but we close early.

Ask: What time?

¿A qué hora?
ah kay orah

Sí, el elevador está allí.
see, el elaybador estah ah-yee

Yes, there's an elevator over there.

Gracias, quisiera cuatro entradas.
grasyas, keesyairah kwatroh entradas

Thank you. I'd like four admission tickets.

Aquí tiene, y la guía es gratis.
ahkee tyenay, ee lah gheeah es gratees

Here you are, and the guidebook is free.

Say "one-thirty."
(pp.30–1)

What's the Spanish for
"ticket"? (pp.38–9)

Say "I am going to
Lima." (pp.40–1)

En el aeropuerto
At the airport

Although the airport environment
is largely international, it is
sometimes useful to be able to ask
your way around the terminal in
Spanish. It's a good idea to make sure
you have some change when you
arrive at the airport; you may need
to give a few tips.

2 Words to remember

Familiarize yourself with these words and test yourself using the flap.

la facturación lah faktoorasyon	*check-in*
las salidas las saleedas	*departures*
las llegadas las yehgadas	*arrivals*
la aduana lah adwanah	*customs*
el control de pasaportes el kontrol day pasaportes	*passport control*
la terminal lah termeenal	*terminal*
la puerta de embarque lah pwertah day embarkay	*boarding gate*

**¿Cuál es la puerta de
embarque para el
vuelo veintitrés?**
kwal es lah pwertah day
embarkay parah el
bweloh beynteetres
*Which is the boarding
gate for Flight 23?*

3 Useful phrases

Learn these phrases and then test yourself using the cover flap.

¿Sale a tiempo el vuelo para Lima? salay ah tyempoh el bweloh parah leemah	*Is the flight to Lima on time?*
No encuentro mi equipaje. noh enkwentroh mee ehkeepahay	*I can't find my luggage.*

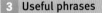

4 Put into practice

Join in this conversation. Read the Spanish on the left and follow
the instructions to make your reply. Then test yourself by concealing
the answers with the cover flap.

Hola, ¿le puedo ayudar?
o-lah, lay pwedoh ahyoodar
Hello, can I help you?

Ask: Is the flight to Quito on time?

¿Sale a tiempo el vuelo para Quito?
salay ah tyempoh el bweloh parah keetoh

Sí señor.
see senyor
Yes, sir.

Ask: Which is the boarding gate?

¿Cuál es la puerta de embarque?
kwal es lah pwertah day embarkay

5 Match and repeat

Match the numbered items to the Spanish words in the panel.

boarding pass ❶

check-in desk ❷

ticket ❸

passport ❹

suitcase ❺   *carry-on luggage* ❻   *cart* ❼

1 **la tarjeta de embarque**
lah tarhetah day embarkay

2 **el mostrador de facturación**
el mostrador day faktoorasyon

3 **el boleto**
el bolaytoh

4 **el pasaporte**
el pasaportay

5 **la maleta**
lah malaytah

6 **el equipaje de mano**
el ehkeepahay day manoh

7 **el carrito**
el karreetoh

Repase y repita
Review and repeat

1 Places

1 **el museo**
el moo<u>say</u>oh

2 **el ayuntamiento**
el ahyoonta-
<u>myain</u>toh

3 **el puente**
el <u>pwen</u>tay

4 **la biblioteca**
lah beeblee-
oh<u>te</u>kah

5 **el estacionamiento**
el estasyona-
<u>myain</u>toh

6 **la catedral**
lah kate<u>dral</u>

7 **la plaza**
lah <u>pla</u>sah

1 Places

Name the numbered places in Spanish.

1 *museum* 2 *town hall* 3 *bridge*

4 *library* 5 *parking lot* 6 *cathedral*

7 *square*

2 Car parts

1 **el parabrisas**
el para<u>bree</u>sas

2 **la directional**
lah deerek<u>syo</u>nal

3 **el cofre**
el <u>kof</u>ray

4 **la llanta**
lah <u>yan</u>tah

5 **la puerta**
lah <u>pwer</u>tah

6 **el parachoques**
el para<u>cho</u>kes

2 Car parts

Name these car parts in Spanish.

windshield 1

4 *tire* 5 *door*

3 Questions

Ask the questions that match these answers.

1 **El autobús sale a las ocho.**
el aootoboos salay ah las ochoh

2 **El café es uno cincuenta.**
el kafay es oonoh seenkwentah

3 **No, no quiero vino.**
noh, noh kyairoh beenoh

4 **El tren sale del andén cinco.**
el tren salay del anden seenkoh

5 **Nosotros vamos a Nuevo León.**
nosotros bamos ah nweboh leh-on

6 **El tren para Santiago es dentro de quince minutos.**
el tren parah santeeahgoh es dentroh day keensay meenootos

3 Questions

1 **¿A qué hora sale el autobús?**
ah kay orah salay el aootoboos

2 **¿Cuánto es el café?**
kwantoh es el kafay

3 **¿Quieres vino?**
kyaires beenoh

4 **¿De qué andén sale el tren?**
day kay anden salay el tren

5 **¿A dónde van?**
ah donday ban

6 **¿Cuándo es el tren para Santiago?**
kwandoh es el tren parah santeeagoh

4 Verbs

Choose the correct form of the verb in brackets to fill in the blanks.

1 **Yo _____ inglés.**
(ser)

2 **Nosotros _____ el metro.** (tomar)

3 **Ella _____ a Lima.** (ir)

4 **Él _____ casado.** (estar)

5 **¿Tú _____ un té?** (querer)

6 **¿Cuántos niños _____ usted?** (tener)

2 *turn signal*

3 *hood*

6 *bumper*

4 Verbs

1 **soy**
soy

2 **tomamos**
tomamos

3 **va**
bah

4 **está**
estah

5 **quieres**
kyaires

6 **tiene**
tyenay

1 Warm up

Ask "Do you take credit cards?" (pp.38–9)

Ask "How much is that?" (pp.18–19)

Ask "Do you have children?" (pp.12–13)

Reservar una habitación
Booking a room

Types of accommodation in Latin America include: **hotel**, categorized from one to five stars; **pensión**, a small family-run hotel; **casa de huéspedes**, cheap and basic; and **haciendas**, old properties converted into luxury hotels.

2 Useful phrases

Practice these phrases and then test yourself by concealing the Spanish on the left with the cover flap.

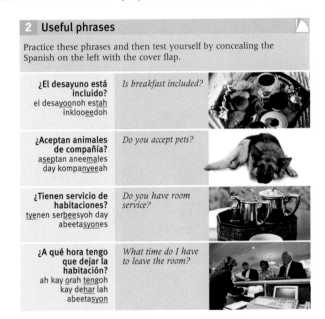

¿El desayuno está incluido?
el desa<u>yoo</u>noh es<u>tah</u> inkloo<u>ee</u>doh

Is breakfast included?

¿Aceptan animales de compañía?
a<u>sep</u>tan anee<u>ma</u>les day kompan<u>yee</u>ah

Do you accept pets?

¿Tienen servicio de habitaciones?
t<u>ye</u>nen ser<u>bee</u>syoh day abeeta<u>sy</u>ones

Do you have room service?

¿A qué hora tengo que dejar la habitación?
ah kay <u>o</u>rah <u>ten</u>goh kay de<u>har</u> lah abeeta<u>sy</u>on

What time do I have to leave the room?

3 In conversation

¿Tiene habitaciones libres?
t<u>ye</u>nay abeeta<u>sy</u>ones <u>lee</u>bres

Do you have any vacancies?

Sí, una habitación doble.
see, <u>oo</u>nah abeeta<u>sy</u>on <u>do</u>blay

Yes, a double room.

¿Tiene una cuna?
t<u>ye</u>nay <u>oo</u>nah <u>koo</u>nah

Do you have a crib?

4 Words to remember

Familiarize yourself with these words and test yourself by concealing the Spanish on the right with the cover flap.

room	**la habitación** lah abeetasyon
single room	**la habitación individual** lah abeetasyon indeebeedwal
double room	**la habitación doble** lah abeetasyon doblay
bathroom	**el baño** el banyoh
shower	**la regadera** lah regaderah
breakfast	**el desayuno** el desayoonoh
key	**la llave** lah yabay
balcony	**el balcón** el balkon
air-conditioning	**el aire acondicionado** el ah-eeray akondeesyonadoh

¿Tiene la habitación vista al parque?
tyenay lah abeetasyon beesta al parkay
Does the room have a view over the park?

5 Say it

Do you have a single room, please?

For six nights.

Is breakfast included?

Cultural tip Large hotels and "haciendas" are generally the only types of hotels to offer breakfast, but you will generally be charged extra. If your accommodation doesn't provide breakfast, you'll usually find a bar or a café nearby where you can go for "café con leche" and a snack in the mornings.

Sí, claro. ¿Cuántas noches?
see, klaroh. kwantas noches

Yes, of course. How many nights?

Para tres noches.
parah tres noches

For three nights.

Muy bien. Aquí tiene la llave.
mwee byen. ahkee tyenay lah yabay

Fine. Here's the key.

1 Warm up

Say "Is there...?" and "There isn't...".
(pp.48–9)

What does "¿Le puedo ayudar?" mean?
(pp.54–5)

En el hotel
In the hotel

Although the larger hotels almost always have private bathrooms, there are still some **pensiones** and **hostels** where you will have to share bathroom facilities and which sometimes don't provide towels. It is always advisable to check what is provided when you book.

2 Match and repeat

Match the numbered items in this hotel bedroom with the Spanish text in the panel and test yourself using the cover flap.

1. **la mesita de noche**
   lah me<u>see</u>yah day <u>no</u>chay

2. **la lámpara**
   lah <u>lam</u>parah

3. **el equipo de música**
   el e<u>kee</u>poh day <u>moo</u>seekah

4. **las cortinas**
   las kor<u>tee</u>nas

5. **el sofá**
   el so<u>fah</u>

6. **la almohada**
   lah almoh-<u>ah</u>dah

7. **el cojín**
   el ko<u>heen</u>

8. **la cama**
   lah <u>ka</u>mah

9. **la colcha**
   lah <u>kol</u>chah

10. **la manta**
    lah <u>man</u>tah

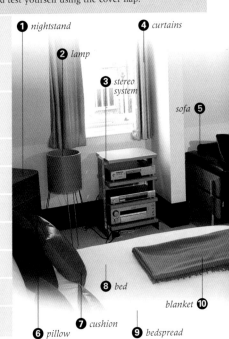

1. nightstand
2. lamp
3. stereo system
4. curtains
5. sofa
6. pillow
7. cushion
8. bed
9. bedspread
10. blanket

Cultural tip If you don't want to share your bed, you'll have to ask for "una habitación doble con dos camas" (a double room with two beds) to get a twin room. Otherwise you will probably get a double bed ("cama de matrimonio" or marriage bed). You should also be aware that cheaper hotels in some parts of Latin America may not have hot running water and you may need to request pillows.

3 Useful phrases

Practice these phrases and then test yourself using the cover flap.

The room is too cold/hot.

Hace demasiado frío/calor en la habitación.
ahsay daymas<u>yah</u>doh freeoh/kalor en lah abeeta<u>syon</u>

There are no towels.

No hay toallas.
noh ah-ee toh-<u>ah</u>yas

I need some soap.

Necesito jabón.
nese<u>see</u>toh ha<u>bon</u>

The shower doesn't work.

La regadera no funciona.
lah rega<u>de</u>rah noh foon<u>syo</u>nah

The elevator is broken.

El elevador está descompuesto.
el elayba<u>dor</u> es<u>tah</u> deskom<u>pwes</u>toh

4 Put into practice

Practice these phrases and then complete the dialogue in Spanish.

¿Ya le atienden?
yah lay at<u>yain</u>den
Can I help you?

Say: I need some pillows.

Necesito almohadas.
nese<u>see</u>toh almoh-<u>ah</u>das

La recamarera se las llevará.
lah raykamar<u>ai</u>rah say las yeb<u>ar</u>ah
The maid will bring some.

Say: And the TV doesn't work.

Y la televisión no funciona.
ee lah telebee<u>syon</u> noh foon<u>syo</u>nah

En el campamento
At the campground

Organized campgrounds are mainly found in Argentina, Uruguay, Chile, and Costa Rica. In other parts of Latin America, camping is more often a specialist activity connected with hiking and mountaineering, for which you need to be well informed and equipped.

2 Useful phrases

Learn these phrases. Then test yourself by concealing the Spanish with the cover flap.

¿Puedo alquilar una bicicleta? pwedoh alkeelar oonah beeseekletah	*Can I rent a bicycle?*
¿El agua es potable? el ahgwah es potablay	*Is this drinking water?*
¿Se permiten fogatas? say permeeten fogatas	*Are campfires allowed?*
Las radios están prohibidas. las rradyos estan proheebeedas	*Radios are forbidden.*

¿Dónde está la llave?
donday estah la yabay
Where is the faucet?

la oficina
lah ofeeseenah
office

el contenedor de la basura
el kontenedor day lah basoorah
trash can

el doble techo
el doblay taychoh
flysheet

3 In conversation

Necesito una plaza para tres noches.
neseseetoh oonah plasah parah tres noches

I need a site for three nights.

Hay una cerca de la piscina.
ah-ee oonah serkah day lah peesseenah

There's one near the swimming pool.

¿Cuánto cuesta para una camioneta?
kwantoh kwestah parah oonah kamyonaytah

How much is it for a camper?

4 Words to remember

Familiarize yourself with these words and test yourself using the flap.

5 Say it

I need a site for four nights.

Can I rent a tent?

Where's the electrical hookup?

campsite	**el campamento** el kampamentoh
tent	**la tienda** lah tyendah
camper trailer	**la camioneta** lah kamyonaytah
camper van	**la autocaravana** la ah-ootokarabanah
site	**la plaza** lah plasah
campfire	**la fogata** lah fogatah
drinking water	**el agua potable** el ahgwah potablay
garbage	**la basura** lah basoorah
stove fuel	**el camping-gas** el kampeen gas
showers	**las regaderas** las regaderas
sleeping bag	**el saco de dormir** el sakoh day dormeer
air mattress	**la colchoneta** lah kolchonetah
groundsheet	**el suelo aislante** el sweloh ah-eeslantay

los baños
los banyos
restrooms

la toma de luz
el tomah day loos
electrical hookup

la cuerda
lah kwerdah
guy rope

la clavija
la klabeehah
tent peg

Cincuenta pesos. Una noche por adelantado.
seenkwentah paysos. oonah nochay por adelantadoh

Fifty pesos. One night in advance.

¿Puedo alquilar un asador?
pwedoh alkeelar oon asador

Can I rent a barbecue grill?

Sí, pero tiene que dejar un depósito.
see, peroh tyenay kay dehar oon deposeetoh

Yes, but you must pay a deposit.

1 Warm up

How do you say "hot" and "cold"? (pp.60–1)

What is the Spanish for "room," "bed," and "pillow"? (pp.60–1)

Descripciones
Descriptions

Adjectives are words used to describe things. In Spanish, you generally put the adjective after the thing it describes in the same gender and number: **una bebida fría** (*a cold drink*, feminine singular); **un café frío** (*a cold coffee*, masculine singular); **dos bebidas frías** (*two cold drinks*, feminine plural).

2 Words to remember

Adjectives change depending on whether the thing described is masculine (**el**) or feminine (**la**). Generally, a final "o" changes to "a" in the feminine, but if the adjective ends with "e" (such as **grande**) it doesn't change for the feminine. For the plural, just add an "s."

duro/dura <u>doo</u>roh/<u>doo</u>rah	*hard*
blando/blanda <u>blan</u>doh/<u>blan</u>dah	*soft*
caliente kal<u>yain</u>tay	*hot*
frío/fría <u>free</u>oh/<u>free</u>ah	*cold*
grande <u>gran</u>day	*big*
pequeño/pequeña pe<u>ken</u>yoh/pe<u>ken</u>yah	*small*
bonito/bonita bo<u>nee</u>toh/bo<u>nee</u>tah	*beautiful*
feo/fea <u>feh</u>-oh/<u>feh</u>-ah	*ugly*
ruidoso/ruidosa rrwee<u>do</u>soh/rrwee<u>do</u>- sah	*noisy*
tranquilo/tranquila tran<u>kee</u>loh/tran<u>kee</u>lah	*quiet*
bueno/buena <u>bwe</u>noh/<u>bwe</u>nah	*good*
malo/mala <u>ma</u>loh/<u>ma</u>lah	*bad*
lento/lenta <u>len</u>toh/<u>len</u>tah	*slow*
rápido/rápida <u>rra</u>peedoh/<u>rra</u>peedah	*fast*

las montañas altas
las mon<u>tan</u>yas <u>al</u>tas
high mountains

**la tienda
pequeña**
lah <u>tyain</u>dah
pe<u>ken</u>yah
small shop

el coche viejo
el <u>ko</u>chay bee-<u>ay</u>hoh
old car

la calle tranquila
lah <u>ka</u>yay tran<u>kee</u>lah
quiet road

**El pueblo es muy
bonito.**
el <u>pwe</u>bloh es mwee
bo<u>nee</u>toh
*The village is very
beautiful.*

3 Useful phrases

Learn these phrases. Note that you can emphasize a description by using **muy** (*very*), **demasiado** (*too*), or **más** (*more*) before the adjective.

	This coffee is cold.	**Este café está frío.** estay kafay estah freeoh
	My room is very noisy.	**Mi habitación es muy ruidosa.** mee abeetasyon es mwee rrweedosah
	My car is too small.	**Mi coche es demasiado pequeño.** mee kochay es demasyahdoh pekenyoh
	I need a softer bed.	**Necesito una cama más blanda.** neseseetoh oonah kamah mas blandah

4 Put into practice

Join in this conversation. Cover up the text on the right and complete the dialogue in Spanish. Check and repeat if necessary.

Ésta es la habitación.
estah es lah
abeetasyon
This is the bedroom.

Say: The view is very beautiful.

La vista es muy bonita.
lah beestah es mwee
boneetah

El baño está por ahí.
el banyoh estah por
ah-ee
The bathroom is over there.

Say: It is too small.

Es demasiado pequeño.
es demasyahdoh
pekenyoh

No tenemos otra.
noh tenaymos otrah
We don't have another one.

Say: It doesn't matter. We'll take the room.

No importa. Nos quedamos con la habitación.
noh importah. nos
kedamos kon lah
abeetasyon

Repase y repita
Review and repeat

1 Descriptions

1 **caliente**
kalyaintay

2 **pequeña**
pekenyah

3 **frío**
free-oh

4 **grande**
granday

5 **tranquila**
trankeelah

1 Descriptions

Put the word in brackets into Spanish. Use the correct masculine or feminine form.

1 El agua está demasiado _____ (hot).

2 La cama es muy _____ (small).

3 El café está _____ (cold).

4 Este baño es más _____ (big).

5 Quisiera una habitación más _____ (quiet).

2 Campground

1 **la toma de luz**
lah tomah day loos

2 **la tienda**
lah tyaindah

3 **el contenedor de la basura**
el kontenedor day lah basoorah

4 **la cuerda**
lah kwerdah

5 **los baños**
los banyos

6 **la camioneta**
lah kamyonaytah

2 Campground

Name these items you might find in a campground:

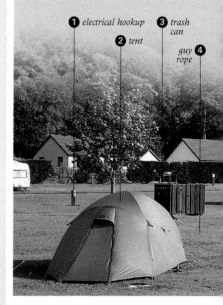

1 electrical hookup
2 tent
3 trash can
4 guy rope

3 At the hotel

You are booking a room in a hotel. Follow the conversation, replying in Spanish where you see the English prompts.

¿Qué desean?
1 *Do you have any vacancies?*

Sí, una habitación doble.
2 *Do you accept pets?*

Sí. ¿Cuántas noches?
3 *Three nights.*

Son ciento cuarenta pesos.
4 *Is breakfast included?*

Sí. Aquí tiene la llave.
5 *Thank you very much.*

3 At the hotel

1 **¿Tiene habitaciones libres?**
tyenay abeeta-syones leebres

2 **¿Aceptan animales de compañía?**
aseptan aneemales day kompanyeeah

3 **Tres noches.**
tres noches

4 **¿El desayuno está incluido?**
el desayoonoh estah inklooeedoh

5 **Muchas gracias.**
moochas grasyas

5 *restrooms*

6 *camper*

4 Negatives

Make these sentences negative using the verb in brackets.

1 Yo ____ hijos. (tener)

2 Ellos ____ a Córdoba mañana. (ir)

3 Él ____ un café. (querer)

4 Yo ____ el metro. (tomar)

5 La vista ____ muy bonita. (ser)

4 Negatives

1 **no tengo**
noh tengoh

2 **no van**
noh ban

3 **no quiere**
noh kyairay

4 **no tomo**
noh tomoh

5 **no es**
no es

De compras
Shopping

Small, traditional shops are still very common in Latin America. But there are also big supermarkets and shopping centers on the outskirts of cities. Local markets selling fresh, local produce can be found everywhere. Ask which day is market day at the **oficina de información turística** (*tourist office*).

2 Match and repeat

Match the stores numbered 1 to 9 below and right to the Spanish in the panel. Then test yourself using the cover flap.

1 **la panadería**
lah panadair<u>ee</u>ah

2 **la pastelería**
lah pastaylair<u>ee</u>ah

3 **la miscelánea**
lah meesel<u>a</u>neah

4 **la carnicería**
lah karnee-sair<u>ee</u>ah

5 **la salchichonería**
lah salcheecho-nair<u>ee</u>ah

6 **la librería**
lah leebrair<u>ee</u>ah

7 **la pescadería**
lah peskadair<u>ee</u>ah

8 **la joyería**
lah hoyer<u>ee</u>ah

9 **el banco**
el <u>ban</u>koh

 ❶ bread shop

 ❷ bakery

 ❹ butcher

 ❺ delicatessen

 ❼ fishmonger

 ❽ jeweler

Cultural tip If you want a bar of soap, a tube of toothpaste, or other toiletries you can go to a "droguería" (drugstore) or a "farmacia" (pharmacy). It is advisable to bring any special items with you because they may not be easy to find. The "miscelánea" is the equivalent of the small corner store. "Papelerías" sell stationery. Many stores offer a free gift-wrapping service; you only need to ask: "¿Me lo envuelve para regalo?" (May I have it gift-wrapped?).

Words to remember

Familiarize yourself with these words and test yourself using the flap.

¿Dónde está la florería?
<u>don</u>day es<u>tah</u> lah florai<u>ree</u>ah
Where is the florist?

hardware store	**la ferretería** lah ferreretai<u>ree</u>ah
antique shop	**el anticuario** el antee<u>kwar</u>eeoh
hairdresser	**la peluquería** lah pelookai<u>ree</u>ah
greengrocer	**la verdulería** lah berdoolai<u>ree</u>ah
post office	**la oficina de correos** lah ofee<u>see</u>nah day <u>korr</u>ayos
shoe store	**la zapatería** lah sapatai<u>ree</u>ah
dry-cleaner	**la tintorería** lah teentorai<u>ree</u>ah
grocery	**los abarrotes** los aba<u>rr</u>otes

❸ *corner store*

❻ *bookstore*

❾ *bank*

Useful phrases

Familiarize yourself with these phrases.

Where is the hairdresser?	**¿Dónde está la peluquería?** <u>don</u>day es<u>tah</u> lah pelookai<u>ree</u>ah
Where do I pay?	**¿Dónde se paga?** <u>don</u>day say <u>pag</u>ah
I'm just looking, thank you.	**Sólo estoy mirando, gracias.** <u>sol</u>oh es<u>toy</u> mee<u>ran</u>doh, <u>gras</u>yas
Do you sell phone cards?	**¿Tiene tarjetas telefónicas?** <u>tye</u>nay tar<u>het</u>as telefo<u>nee</u>kas
May I have two of those?	**¿Me da dos de éstos?** may dah dos day <u>est</u>os
Can I place an order?	**¿Puedo hacer un pedido?** <u>pwe</u>doh ah<u>ser</u> oon pe<u>dee</u>doh

Say it

Where is the bank?

Do you sell cheese?

Where do I pay?

What is Spanish for "40," "56," "77," "82," and "94"? (pp.10–11, pp.30–1)

Say "I'd like a big room." (pp.64–5)

Ask "Do you have a small car?" (pp.64–5)

En el mercado
At the market

Latin America uses the metric system of weights and measures. You need to ask for produce in kilograms or grams. Some larger items such as melons or pineapples tend to be sold by **la pieza** (as single items); other items, such as lettuces, may be sold in lots of two or three.

2 Match and repeat

Match the numbered items in this scene with the text in the panel.

1 **los jitomates**
los heeto**mates**

2 **los ejotes**
los e**ho**tes

3 **los hongos**
los **on**gos

4 **las uvas**
las **oo**bas

5 **los pepinos**
los pe**pee**nos

6 **las alcachofas**
las alka**cho**fas

7 **los chícharos**
los **chee**charos

8 **los pimientos**
los pee**myain**tos

1 tomatoes

5 cucumbers

artichokes 6

peas 7

peppers 8

3 In conversation

Quisiera jitomates.
kees**yair**ah heeto**mates**

I'd like some tomatoes.

¿De los grandes o de los pequeños?
day los **gran**des oh day los pe**ken**yos

The large ones or the small ones?

Dos kilos de los pequeños, por favor.
dos **kee**los day los pe**ken**yos, por fa**bor**

Two kilos of the small ones, please.

Cultural tip Argentina, Chile, Uruguay, Colombia, and Mexico all call their currency the peso. Other currencies are: Bolivia, boliviano; Venezuela, bolívar; Perú, nuevo sol; Nicaragua, córdoba; Guatemala, quetzal. Most of them divide into 100 centavos.

❷ *beans*

❸ *mushrooms*

❹ *grapes*

4 Useful phrases

Learn these phrases. Then cover up the answers on the right. Read the English under the pictures and say the phrase in Spanish as shown on the right.

Esa salchicha es demasiado cara.
ehsah salcheechah es demasyahdoh karah

That sausage is too expensive.

¿A cuánto está ese?
ah kwantoh estah ehsay

How much is that one?

5 Say it

Three kilos of grapes, please.

The mushrooms are too expensive.

How much are the beans?

Eso es todo.
ehsoh es todoh

That's all.

¿Algo más, señorita?
algoh mas, senyoreetah

Anything else, miss?

Eso es todo, gracias. ¿Cuánto es?
ehsoh es todoh, grasyas. kwantoh es

That's all, thank you. How much?

Diez cincuenta.
dee-es seenkwentah

Ten-fifty.

1 Warm up

What are these items you could buy in a supermarket? (pp.24–5)

la carne
el pescado
el queso
el jugo
el vino
el agua

En el supermercado
At the supermarket

Supermarkets are usually cheaper than smaller shops. They offer all kinds of products, including clothes and household goods. Prices, however, may be higher than in local markets, which also offer a wide range of goods.

2 Match and repeat

Look at the numbered product categories and match them to the Spanish words in the panel on the left. Test yourself using the flap.

1 **los productos del hogar**
los pro<u>dook</u>tos del oh<u>gar</u>

2 **la fruta**
lah <u>froo</u>tah

3 **las bebidas**
las be<u>bee</u>das

4 **los platos preparados**
los <u>pla</u>tos prepa<u>ra</u>dos

5 **los productos de belleza**
los pro<u>dook</u>tos day be<u>ye</u>sah

6 **los productos lácteos**
los pro<u>dook</u>tos <u>lak</u>teh-os

7 **la verdura**
lah ber<u>doo</u>rah

8 **los congelados**
los konhe<u>la</u>dos

household products ❶

fruit ❷

drinks ❸

prepared meals ❹

vegetables ❼

frozen foods ❽

Cultural tip It is not always possible to take unweighed fruit and vegetables sold by the kilo directly to the supermarket checkout. There is often a separate counter or a self-service weighing machine.

3 Useful phrases

Learn these phrases and then test yourself using the cover flap.

May I have a bag, please?
¿Me da una bolsa, por favor?
may dah <u>oo</u>nah <u>bol</u>sah, por fa<u>bor</u>

Where are the drinks?
¿Dónde están las bebidas?
<u>don</u>day es<u>tan</u> las be<u>bee</u>das

Where is the checkout, please?
¿Dónde está la caja, por favor?
<u>don</u>day es<u>tah</u> lah <u>ka</u>hah, por fa<u>bor</u>

Please type in your PIN.
Por favor, introduzca su número personal.
por fa<u>bor</u>, intro<u>doo</u>skah soo <u>noo</u>mairoh perso<u>nal</u>

4 Words to remember

Learn these words and then test yourself using the cover flap.

5 *beauty products*

6 *dairy products*

bread	**el pan** el pan	
milk	**la leche** lah <u>le</u>chay	
butter	**la mantequilla** lah mante<u>kee</u>yah	
ham	**el jamón** el ha<u>mon</u>	
salt	**la sal** lah sal	
pepper	**la pimienta** lah pee<u>my</u>aintah	
laundry detergent	**el jabón de lavadora** el ha<u>bon</u> day laba<u>dor</u>ah	
toilet paper	**el papel higiénico** el pa<u>pel</u> eehy<u>ai</u>neekoh	
diapers	**los pañales** los pan<u>ya</u>les	

5 Say it

Where are the dairy products?

May I have some cheese, please?

Where are the frozen foods?

1 Warm up

Say "I'd like...".
(pp.22–3)

Ask "Do you have...?"
(pp.14–15)

Say "38" and "46."
(pp. 10–11 and
pp.30–1)

Say "small," "bigger,"
and "smaller."
(pp.64–5)

La ropa y los zapatos
Clothes and shoes

Clothes and shoes are measured in metric sizes from 36 upward. Even allowing for conversion of sizes, clothes tend to be cut smaller than American ones. Clothes size is **la talla** but shoe size is **el número**.

2 Match and repeat

Match the numbered items to the Spanish words in the panel on the left.

1 **la camisa**
lah kameesah

2 **la corbata**
lah korbatah

3 **el saco**
el sakoh

4 **el bolsillo**
el bolseeyoh

5 **la manga**
lah mangah

6 **el pantalón**
el pantalon

7 **la falda**
lah faldah

8 **las medias**
las medyas

9 **los zapatos**
los sapatos

shirt ❶

tie ❷

jacket ❸

pocket ❹

sleeve ❺

pants ❻

Cultural tip Latin America uses the continental (European) system of sizes. Women's clothes sizes usually range from 36 (US 6) through to 46 (US 18), and shoe sizes from 37 (US 6) to 45 (US 12). For men's shirts, a size 41 is a 16-inch collar, 43 is a 17-inch collar, and 45 is an 18-inch collar.

3 Useful phrases

Practice these phrases and then test yourself using the cover flap.

Do you have a bigger size?	**¿Tiene una talla más grande?** tyenay oonah tayah mas granday
It's not what I want.	**No es lo que quiero.** noh es loh kay kyairoh
I'll take the pink one.	**Me quedo con el rosa.** may kedoh kon el rrosah

4 Words to remember

Colors are adjectives (pp.64–5) and in most cases have a masculine and a feminine form. The feminine is usually formed by substituting an "a" for the final "o."

red	**rojo/roja** rrohoh/rrohah
white	**blanco/blanca** blankoh/blankah
blue	**azul** asool
yellow	**amarillo/amarilla** amareeyoh/amareeyah
green	**verde** berday
black	**negro/negra** negroh/negrah

7 *skirt*

8 *pantyhose*

9 *shoes*

5 Say it

What shoe size?

Do you have a black jacket?

Do you have a size 38?

Do you have a smaller size?

Respuestas
Answers
Cover with flap

Repase y repita
Review and repeat

Market

1 Market

Name the numbered vegetables in Spanish.

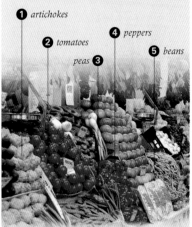

❶ artichokes
❹ peppers
❷ tomatoes
❺ beans
peas ❸

Respuestas — Market

1 **los alcachofas**
los alka<u>cho</u>fas

2 **los jitomates**
los heeto<u>ma</u>tes

3 **los chícharos**
los <u>chee</u>charos

4 **los pimientos**
los pee<u>myain</u>tos

5 **los ejotes**
los e<u>ho</u>tes

Description

2 Description

What do these sentences mean?

1 Los zapatos son demasiados caros.

2 Mi habitación es muy pequeña.

3 Necesito una cama más blanda.

Respuestas — Description

1 *The shoes are too expensive.*

2 *My room is very small.*

3 *I need a softer bed.*

Stores

3 Stores

Name the numbered stores in Spanish.
Then check your answers.

❶ bread shop ❷ jeweler ❸ bookstore

❹ fishmonger ❺ bakery ❻ butcher

Respuestas — Stores

1 **la panadería**
lah panadai<u>ree</u>ah

2 **la joyería**
lah hoyeh<u>ree</u>ah

3 **la librería**
lah leebrai<u>ree</u>ah

4 **la pescadería**
lah peskadai<u>ree</u>ah

5 **la pastelería**
lah pastaylai<u>ree</u>ah

6 **la carnicería**
lah karneesai<u>ree</u>ah

Supermarket

What is the Spanish for the numbered product categories?

1 *household products*

2 *beauty products*

3 *drinks*

4 *dairy products*

5 *vegetables*

Supermarket

1 **los productos del hogar**
los pro<u>dook</u>tos del oh<u>gar</u>

2 **los productos de belleza.**
los pro<u>dook</u>tos day be<u>ye</u>sah

3 **las bebidas**
las be<u>bee</u>das

4 **los productos lácteos**
los pro<u>dook</u>tos <u>lak</u>teh-os

5 **la verdura**
lah ber<u>doo</u>rah

Museum

Follow this conversation, replying in Spanish following the English prompts.

Buenos días. ¿Qué desean?
1 *I'd like five tickets.*

Son setenta y cinco pesos.
2 *That's very expensive!*

No hacemos descuentos a los niños.
3 *How much is a guide?*

Quince pesos.
4 *Good. And five tickets, please.*

Noventa pesos, por favor.
5 *Here you are. Where are the restrooms?*

A la derecha.
6 *Thank you very much.*

Museum

1 **Quisiera cinco entradas.**
kee<u>sya</u>irah <u>seen</u>koh en<u>tra</u>das

2 **¡Es muy caro!**
es mwe <u>ka</u>roh

3 **¿Cuánto cuesta una guía?**
<u>kwan</u>toh <u>kwes</u>tah <u>oo</u>nah <u>ghee</u>ah

4 **Bien. Y cinco entradas, por favor.**
Byen. ee <u>seen</u>koh en<u>tra</u>das, por fa<u>bor</u>

5 **Aquí tiene. ¿Dónde están los baños?**
ah<u>kee</u> <u>tye</u>nay. <u>don</u>day es<u>tan</u> los <u>ban</u>yos

6 **Muchas gracias.**
<u>moo</u>chas <u>gra</u>syas

Las ocupaciones
Occupations

1 Warm up

Say "from which platform?" (pp.38–9)

What is the Spanish for the following family members: sister, brother, mother, father, son, and daughter? (pp.10–11)

Some occupations have commonly used feminine alternatives—for example, **enfermero** (*male nurse*) and **enfermera** (*female nurse*). Others remain the same. When you describe your occupation, you don't use **un/una** (*a*), saying simply **soy abogado** (*I'm a lawyer*), for example.

2 Words to remember: jobs

Familiarize yourself with these words and test yourself using the cover flap. The feminine ending is also shown.

médico mehdeekoh	*doctor*
dentista denteestah	*dentist*
enfermero/-a enfermairoh/-ah	*nurse*
profesor/-sora profaysor/-sorah	*teacher*
contador/-a kontador/-ah	*accountant*
abogado/-a abogadoh/-ah	*lawyer*
diseñador/-dora deesenyador/-dorah	*designer*
consultor/-a konsooltor/-torah	*consultant*
secretario/-a sekraytareeoh/-ah	*secretary*
comerciante komersyantay	*shopkeeper*
electricista elektreeseestah	*electrician*
plomero/-a plomairoh/-ah	*plumber*
cocinero/-a koseenairoh/-ah	*cook/chef*
albañil albanyeel	*handyman*
autónomo/-a aootohnomoh/-ah	*self-employed*

Soy plomero.
 soy plomairoh
 I'm a plumber.

Es estudiante.
 es estoodyantay
 She is a student.

3 Put into practice

Join in this conversation. Read the Spanish on the left and follow the instructions to make your reply. Then test yourself.

¿Cuál es su profesión?
kwal es soo profesyon
What do you do?

Say: I am a consultant.

Soy consultor.
soy konsooltor

¿Para qué empresa trabaja?
parah kay empresah trabahah
What company do you work for?

Say: I'm self-employed.

Soy autónomo.
soy aootohnomoh

¡Qué interesante!
kay intairaysantay
How interesting!

Say: And what is your profession?

¿Y cuál es su profesión?
ee kwal es soo profesyon

Soy dentista.
soy denteestah
I'm a dentist.

Say: My sister is a dentist, too.

Mi hermana es dentista también.
mee airmanah es denteestah tambyen

---

4 Words to remember: workplace

Familiarize yourself with these words and test yourself.

La oficina central está en la capital.
lah ofeeseenah sentral estah en lah kapeetal
Headquarters is in the capital.

branch	**la sucursal** lah sookoorsal
department	**el departamento** el departamaintoh
manager	**el jefe** el hefay
employee	**el empleado** el emplay-ahdoh
reception	**la recepción** lah rresepsyon
trainee	**el aprendiz** el ahprendees

1 Warm up

Practice different ways of introducing yourself in different situations (pp.8–9). Mention your name, occupation (pp.78–9), and any other information you'd like to volunteer.

La oficina
The office

An office environment or business situation has its own vocabulary in any language, but there are items that are virtually universal. Be aware that Spanish-language keyboards have a different layout from the standard "QWERTY" convention; they also include **ñ**, vowels with accents, **¡**, and **¿**.

2 Words to remember

Familiarize yourself with these words. Read them aloud several times and try to memorize them. Conceal the Spanish with the cover flap and test yourself.

el monitor el mon**ee**tor	*monitor*
el ratón el rr**a**ton	*mouse*
el correo electrónico el korrayoh elektroneekoh	*email*
el internet el eenter**net**	*Internet*
la contraseña lah kontra**sen**yah	*password*
la mensajería de voz lah mensah**ree**ah day bos	*voicemail*
el fax el fax	*fax machine*
la fotocopiadora lah fotokopya**do**rah	*photocopier*
la agenda lah ah-**hen**dah	*planner*
la tarjeta de visita lah tar**het**ah day bee**see**tah	*business card*
la reunión lah reh-oon**yon**	*meeting*
la conferencia lah konfair**en**seeah	*conference*
el orden del día el **or**den del **dee**ah	*agenda*

1 *lamp*

screen **4**

2 *stapler*

telephone **3**

pen **10**

notepad **11**

drawer **12**

3 Useful phrases

Learn these phrases and then test yourself using the flap.

I need to make some photocopies.	**Necesito hacer unas fotocopias.** neseseetoh ahser oonas fotokopyas
I'd like to arrange an appointment.	**Quisiera hacer una cita.** keesyairah ahser oonah seetah
I want to send an email.	**Quiero mandar un correo electrónico.** kyairoh mandar oon korrayoh elektroneekoh

4 Match and repeat

Match the numbered items to the Spanish words on the left.

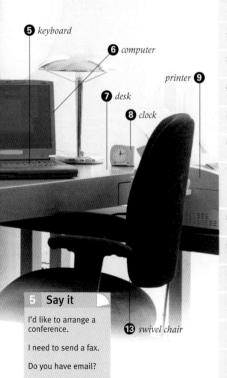

5 *keyboard*
6 *computer*
9 *printer*
7 *desk*
8 *clock*
13 *swivel chair*

1 **la lámpara**
  lah lamparah

2 **la engrapadora**
  lah engrapadorah

3 **el teléfono**
  el telefonoh

4 **la pantalla**
  lah pantayah

5 **el teclado**
  el tekladoh

6 **la computadora**
  lah kompootadorah

7 **la mesa de escritorio**
  lah mesah day eskreetoryoh

8 **el reloj**
  el rrelokh

9 **la impresora**
  lah impresorah

10 **la pluma**
   lah ploomah

11 **el bloc**
   el blok

12 **el cajón**
   el kahon

13 **la silla giratoria**
   lah seeyah heeratoreeah

5 Say it

I'd like to arrange a conference.

I need to send a fax.

Do you have email?

1 Warm up

Say "library" and
"How interesting!".
(pp.48–9, pp.78–9)

Ask "What is your
profession?" and
answer "I'm an
engineer." (pp.78–9)

El mundo académico
Academic world

In the Spanish-speaking world, students
are selected for a first degree (**una
licenciatura**) by an average of school
grades and an exam. After graduation
students, may go on to **un máster**
(master's) or **un doctorado** (PhD).

2 Useful phrases

Practice these phrases and then test yourself using the cover flap.

¿Cuál es su especialidad? kwal es soo espeseeahleedad	*What is your field?*	
Hago investigación en bioquímica. ahgoh inbesteegasyon en beeohkeemeekah	*I'm doing research in biochemistry.*	
Soy licenciado en derecho. soy leesenseeahdoh en derechoh	*I have a degree in law.*	
Voy a dar una conferencia sobre arquitectura. boy ah dar oonah confairaynseeah sobreh arkeetektoorah	*I'm going to give a lecture on architecture.*	

3 In conversation

Hola, soy la profesora Fernández.
ohlah, soy lah profaysorah fernandes

Hello, I'm Professor Fernández.

¿De qué universidad es usted?
deh keh ooneeberseedad es oosted

What university are you from?

De la Universidad de Mérida.
deh lah ooneeberseedad deh maireedah

From the University of Mérida.

4 Words to remember

Familiarize yourself with these words and then test yourself.

conference/lecture	**la conferencia** lah konfair<u>ain</u>seeah
trade fair	**la feria** lah <u>fe</u>reeah
seminar	**el seminario** el semee<u>nary</u>oh
lecture hall	**el anfiteatro** el anfeetay-<u>ah</u>troh
conference room	**la sala de conferencias** lah <u>sah</u>lah deh konfer<u>ain</u>seeas
exhibition	**la exposición** lah eksposees<u>yon</u>
library	**la biblioteca** lah bibleeo<u>te</u>kah
associate professor	**el profesor de universidad** el profay<u>sor</u> deh ooneeber<u>seedad</u>
medicine	**medicina** medee<u>see</u>nah
science	**ciencias** <u>syain</u>seeas
literature	**literatura** leetaira<u>too</u>rah
engineering	**ingeniería** inhenyair<u>ee</u>ah
law	**derecho** de<u>re</u>choh

Tenemos un stand en la feria.
te<u>ne</u>mos oon e<u>stand</u> en la <u>fe</u>reeah
We have a stand at the trade fair.

5 Say it

I'm doing research in medicine.

I have a degree in literature.

She's the professor.

¿Cuál es su especialidad?
kw<u>al</u> es soo espesyalee<u>dad</u>

What's your field?

Hago investigación en ingeniería.
<u>ah</u>goh inbesteegasy<u>on</u> en inhenyair<u>ee</u>ah

I'm doing research in engineering.

¡Qué interesante!
keh intairay<u>san</u>tay!

How interesting!

1 Warm up

Ask "Can I ...?"
(pp.34–5)

Say "I want to send an email." (pp.80–1)

Say "I'd like to make an appointment."
(pp.80–1)

Los negocios
In business

You will receive a more friendly reception and make a good impression if you make the effort to begin a meeting with a short introduction in Spanish, even if your vocabulary is limited. After that, all parties will probably be happy to continue the proceedings in English.

2 Words to remember

Familiarize yourself with these words and then test yourself by concealing the Spanish with the cover flap.

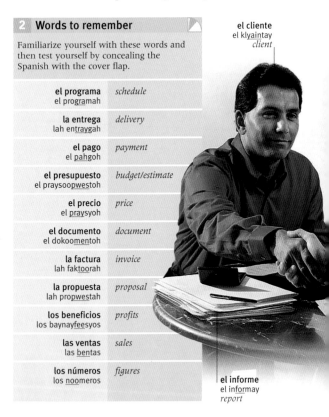

el cliente
el klyaintay
client

el programa el programah	*schedule*
la entrega lah entraygah	*delivery*
el pago el pahgoh	*payment*
el presupuesto el praysoopwestoh	*budget/estimate*
el precio el praysyoh	*price*
el documento el dokoomentoh	*document*
la factura lah faktoorah	*invoice*
la propuesta lah propwestah	*proposal*
los beneficios los baynayfeesyos	*profits*
las ventas las bentas	*sales*
los números los noomeros	*figures*

el informe
el informay
report

Cultural tip A long lunch is still a regular feature of doing business in Latin America. Expect to engage in social talk before getting down to business. As a client, you may be taken out, and as a supplier you should consider entertaining your customers.

3 Useful phrases

Practice these useful business phrases and then test yourself using the cover flap.

¿Firmamos el contrato?
feer<u>ma</u>mos el kon<u>tra</u>toh
Shall we sign the contract?

el ejecutivo
el eh-heekoo<u>tee</u>boh
executive

Please send me the contract.

Me manda el contrato, por favor.
may <u>man</u>dah el kon<u>tra</u>toh, por fa<u>bor</u>

¿Hemos acordado un programa?
<u>eh</u>mos akor<u>da</u>doh oon pro<u>gra</u>mah

Have we agreed on a schedule?

¿Cuándo puede hacer la entrega?
<u>kwan</u>doh <u>pwe</u>day a<u>ser</u> lah en<u>tre</u>gah

When can you make the delivery?

¿Cuál es el presupuesto?
<u>kwal</u> es el praysoo<u>pwes</u>toh

What's the budget?

¿Me puede mandar la factura?
may <u>pwe</u>day man<u>dar</u> lah fak<u>too</u>rah

Can you send me the invoice?

el contrato
el kon<u>tra</u>toh
contract

4 Say it

Can you send me the estimate?

Have we agreed on a price?

What are the profits?

Repase y repita
Review and repeat

1 At the office

1 **la engrapadora**
lah engrapadorah

2 **la lámpara**
lah lamparah

3 **lah computadora**
lah kompootadorah

4 **el bolígrafo**
el boleegrafoh

5 **el reloj**
el rrelokh

6 **el bloc**
el blok

7 **la mesa de escritorio**
lah mesah day eskreetoryoh

1 At the office

Name these items.

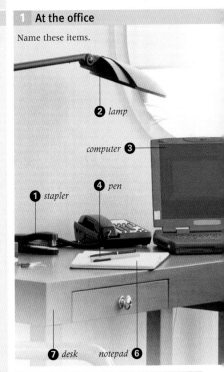

2 *lamp*

computer 3

4 *pen*

1 *stapler*

7 *desk*   *notepad* 6

2 Jobs

1 **médico**
medeekoh

2 **plomero/-a**
plomairoh/-ah

3 **comerciante**
komersyantay

4 **contador**
kontador

5 **estudiante**
estoodyantay

6 **abogado/-a**
abogadoh/-ah

2 Jobs

What are these jobs in Spanish?

1 *doctor*

2 *plumber*

3 *shopkeeper*

4 *accountant*

5 *student*

6 *lawyer*

clock **5**

3 Work

Answer these questions following the English prompts.

¿Para qué empresa trabaja?
1 *Say: I am self-employed.*

¿En qué universidad está?
2 *Say: I'm at the University of Monterrey.*

¿Cuál es su especialidad?
3 *Say: I'm doing research in medicine.*

¿Hemos acordado un programa?
4 *Say: Yes, my secretary has the schedule.*

3 Work

1 **Soy autónomo.**
soy aootonomoh

2 **Estoy en la Universidad de Monterrey.**
estoy en lah ooneeberseedad day montairray

3 **Hago investigación en medicina.**
ahgoh inbesteegasyon en medeeseenah

4 **Sí. mi secretaria tiene el programa.**
see. mee sekretareeah tyenay el programah

4 How much?

Answer the question with the amount in pesos shown in brackets.

1 ¿Cuánto cuesta el desayuno? (10.50)

2 ¿Cuánto cuesta la habitación? (200)

3 ¿Cuánto cuesta un kilo de jitomates? (9.25)

4 ¿Cuánto cuesta un plaza para cuatro noches? (160)

4 How much?

1 **Son diez pesos cincuenta.**
son dee-es paysos seenkwentah

2 **Son doscientos pesos.**
son dos-seeayntos paysos

3 **Son nueve pesos veinticinco.**
son nwebay paysos beynteeseenkoh

4 **Son ciento sesenta pesos.**
son seeayntoh sesentah paysos

1 Warm up

Say "I'm allergic to nuts"). (pp.24–5)

Say the verb "tener" (to have) in all its forms: yo, tú, él/ella, nosotros/-as, ellos/-as). (pp.14–15)

En la farmacia
At the pharmacy

Many pharmacists are qualified to give advice and sell over-the-counter medicines, as well as dispensing prescription medicines. There is generally a **farmacia de guardia** (duty pharmacy) to provide 24-hour service in every town—a list is often displayed in pharmacies.

2 Match and repeat

Match the numbered items to the Spanish words in the panel on the left and test yourself using the cover flap.

1 **la venda**
lah <u>ben</u>dah

2 **el jarabe**
el ha<u>ra</u>bay

3 **las gotas**
las <u>go</u>tas

4 **la curita**
lah koo<u>ree</u>tah

5 **la jeringa**
lah he<u>reen</u>gah

6 **la crema**
lah <u>kre</u>mah

7 **el supositorio**
el sooposee<u>tor</u>yoh

8 **la pastilla**
lah pas<u>tee</u>yah

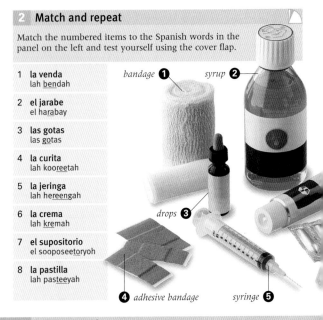

bandage **1**   *syrup* **2**

drops **3**

4 *adhesive bandage*   *syringe* **5**

3 In conversation

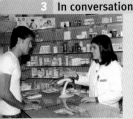

Buenos días, señor. ¿Qué desea?
<u>bwe</u>nos <u>dee</u>yas, sen<u>yor</u>. kay de<u>sa</u>yah

Good morning, sir. What would you like?

Tengo dolor de estómago.
<u>ten</u>goh dolor day es<u>to</u>magoh

I have a stomachache.

¿Tiene diarrea?
<u>tye</u>nay deeah<u>rray</u>ah

Do you have diarrhea?

4 Words to remember

Familiarize yourself with these words and test yourself using the flap.

Tengo dolor de cabeza.
tengoh dolor day kabesah
I have a headache.

headache	**el dolor de cabeza**	el dolor day kabesah
stomachache	**el dolor de estómago**	el dolor day estomagoh
diarrhea	**la diarrea**	lah deeahrrayah
cold	**el resfriado**	el rresfreeahdoh
cough	**la tos**	lah tos
sunburn	**la insolación**	lah eensolaseeyon
toothache	**el dolor de muelas**	el dolor day mwelas

6 Say it

I have a cold.

Do you have that as an ointment?

He has a toothache.

6 *ointment*

7 *suppository*

8 *tablet*

5 Useful phrases

Practice these phrases and then test yourself using the cover flap.

I have a sunburn.	**Tengo una insolación.** tengoh oonah eensolaseeyon
Do you have that as a syrup?	**¿Lo tiene en jarabe?** loh tyenay en harabay
I'm allergic to penicillin.	**Soy alérgico a la penicilina.** soy alerheekoh ah lah peneeseeleenah

No, pero tengo dolor de cabeza.
noh, peroh tengoh dolor day kabesah

No, but I have a headache.

Aquí tiene.
ahkee tyenay

Here you are.

¿Lo tiene en pastilla?
loh tyenay en pasteeyah

Do you have it as tablets?

1 Warm up

Say " I have a toothache" and "I have a sunburn." (pp.88–9)

Say the Spanish for "red," "green," "black," and "yellow." (pp.74–5)

El cuerpo
The body

You are most likely to need to refer to parts of the body in the context of illness—for example, when describing aches and pains to a doctor. The most common phrases for talking about discomfort are **Tengo un dolor en la/el…** *(I have a pain in the…)* and **Me duele la/el…** *(My … hurts)*.

2 Match and repeat: body

Match the numbered parts of the body with the list on the left. Test yourself by using the cover flap.

1 **la mano**
   lah <u>ma</u>noh

2 **la cabeza**
   lah <u>ka</u>besah

3 **el hombro**
   el <u>om</u>broh

4 **el codo**
   el <u>ko</u>doh

5 **el pelo**
   el <u>pe</u>loh

6 **el brazo**
   el <u>bra</u>soh

7 **el cuello**
   el <u>kwe</u>yoh

8 **el pecho**
   el <u>pe</u>choh

9 **el estómago**
   el es<u>to</u>magoh

10 **la pierna**
   lah <u>pyair</u>nah

11 **la rodilla**
   lah rro<u>de</u>eyah

12 **el pie**
   el pee-<u>ay</u>

hand **1**

4 *elbow*

5 *hair*

head **2**

6 *arm*

7 *neck*

8 *chest*

shoulder **3**

9 *stomach*

10 *leg*

11 *knee*

12 *foot*

3 Match and repeat: face

Match the numbered facial features with the list on the right.

eyebrow **1**

nose **3**

2 *eye*

4 *mouth*

ear **5**

1 **la ceja**
  lah <u>say</u>ah

2 **el ojo**
  el <u>oh</u>-hoh

3 **la nariz**
  lah na<u>rees</u>

4 **la boca**
  lah <u>bok</u>ah

5 **la oreja**
  lah oh<u>ray</u>ah

4 Useful phrases

Learn these phrases and then test yourself using the cover flap.

I have a pain in my back.	**Tengo un dolor en la espalda.** <u>ten</u>goh oon do<u>lor</u> en lah es<u>pal</u>da
I have a rash on my arm.	**Tengo un salpullido en el brazo.** <u>ten</u>goh oon salpoo<u>yee</u>doh en el <u>bra</u>soh
I don't feel well.	**No me siento bien.** noh may <u>syen</u>toh byen

5 Put into practice

Join in this conversation and test yourself using the cover flap.

¿Cuál es el problema? kw<u>al</u> es el pro<u>ble</u>mah *What's the problem?* Say: *I don't feel well.*	**No me siento bien.** noh may <u>syen</u>toh byen
¿Dónde le duele? <u>don</u>day lay <u>dwe</u>lay *Where does it hurt?* Say: *I have a pain in my shoulder.*	**Tengo un dolor en el hombro.** <u>ten</u>goh oon do<u>lor</u> en el <u>om</u>broh

En el médico
At the doctor

1 Warm up

Say "I need some tablets." (pp.60–1, pp.88–9)

Say "He needs some cream" (pp.88–9).

What is the Spanish for "I don't have a son." (pp.10–15)

Latin America is a vast region with health hazards that may be unfamiliar to tourists. Be prepared by finding out about the area, having appropriate immunizations, and buying insurance. Unless it's an emergency, you have to make an appointment with a doctor and pay before you leave.

2 Useful phrases you may hear

Practice these phrases and then test yourself using the cover flap to conceal the Spanish on the left.

No es grave. noh es gravay	*It's not serious.*
Necesita hacerse unas pruebas. neseseetah ahsersay oonas prwaybas	*You need to have some tests.*
Tiene una infección de riñón. tyenay oonah infeksyon day rreenyon	*You have a kidney infection.*
Necesita ir al hospital. neseseetah eer al ospeetal	*You need to go to the hospital.*

Le voy a dar una receta. lay boy ah dar oonah rresetah
I'm going to give you a prescription.

3 In conversation

¿Cuál es el problema? kwal es el problemah

What's the problem?

Tengo un dolor en el pecho. tengoh oon dolor en el pechoh

I have a pain in my chest.

Déjeme que la examine. dayhaymay kay lah eksameenay

Let me examine you.

Cultural tip Your hotel, a local pharmacy, or tourist office may be able to put you in touch with a local doctor. In an urgent case it may also be possible to attend a hospital emergency room.

4 Useful phrases you may need to say

Practice these phrases and then test yourself using the cover flap.

I'm diabetic.	**Soy diabético/-a.** soy deeah<u>bet</u>eekoh/-ah
I'm epileptic.	**Soy epiléptico/-a.** soy epee<u>lep</u>teekoh/-ah
I have asthma.	**Soy asmático/-a.** soy as<u>mat</u>eekoh/-ah
I have a heart condition.	**Tengo un problema de corazón.** <u>ten</u>goh oon pro<u>ble</u>mah day kora<u>son</u>
I have a temperature.	**Tengo fiebre.** <u>ten</u>goh <u>fyay</u>bray
I feel faint.	**Estoy mareado.** es<u>toy</u> maray-<u>ah</u>doh
It's urgent.	**Es urgente.** es oor<u>hen</u>tay

Estoy embarazada.
es<u>toy</u> embara<u>sa</u>dah
I'm pregnant.

5 Say it

My son is diabetic.

I have a pain in my arm.

It's not urgent.

¿Es grave?
es <u>gra</u>vay

Is it serious?

No, sólo tiene indigestión.
noh, <u>so</u>loh <u>tye</u>nay indeehesty<u>on</u>

No, you only have indigestion.

¡Menos mal!
<u>may</u>nos mal

What a relief!

1 Warm up

`Say "How long is the trip?" (pp.42–3)

Ask "Is it serious?" (pp.92–3)

What is the Spanish for "mouth" and "head"? (pp.90–1)

En el hospital
At the hospital

It is useful to know a few basic phrases relating to hospitals and medical treatment for use in an emergency or in case you need to visit a friend or colleague in the hospital. Entrance by visitors to hospitals is often controlled. Approach the reception desk first.

2 Useful phrases

Familiarize yourself with these phrases. Conceal the Spanish with the cover flap and test yourself.

¿Cuáles son las horas de visita?
kwales son las oras day beeseetah
What are the visiting hours?

el gotero
el goteroh
drip

¿Cuánto tiempo va a tardar?
kwantoh tyempoh bah ah tardar
How long will it take?

¿Va a doler?
bah ah doler
Will it hurt?

Acuéstese aquí por favor.
akwestesay ahkee por fabor
Please lie down here.

No puede comer nada.
noh pweday komer nadah
You cannot eat anything.

No mueva la cabeza.
noh mwebah lah kabesah
Don't move your head.

¿Se siente mejor?
say syentay mehor
Are you feeling better?

Abra la boca por favor.
ahbrah lah bokah por fabor
Open your mouth, please.

Necesita un análisis de sangre.
neseseetah oon analeesees day sangray
You need a blood test.

¿Dónde está la sala de espera?
donday estah lah salah day esperah
Where is the waiting room?

3 Words to remember

Familiarize yourself with these words and test yourself using the flap.

Su radiografía es normal.
soo rradyografeeah es normal
Your X-ray is normal.

emergency room	**el servicio de urgencias** el serbeesyoh day oorhenseeas
X-ray department	**el servicio de radiología** el serbeesyoh day rradyoloheeah
children's ward	**la sala de pediatría** lah salah day pedeeatreeah
operating room	**el quirófano** el keerofanoh
waiting room	**la sala de espera** lah salah day esperah
stairs	**las escaleras** las eskaleras

4 Put into practice

Join in this conversation. Cover up the text on the right and complete the answering part of the dialogue in Spanish. Check your answers and repeat if necessary.

Tiene una infección.
tyenay oonah infeksyon
You have an infection

Ask: Do I need tests?

¿Necesito hacerme pruebas?
neseseetoh ahsermay prwaybas

Primero necesita un análisis de sangre.
preemeroh neseseetah oon analeesees day sangray
First you will need a blood test.

Ask: Will it hurt?

¿Me va a doler?
may bah ah doler

5 Say it

Does he need a blood test?

Where is the children's ward?

Do I need an X-ray?

No, no se preocupe.
noh, noh say pray-okoopay
No. Don't worry.

Ask: How long will it take?

¿Cuánto tiempo va a tardar?
kwantoh tyempoh bah ah tardar

Respuestas
Answers
Cover with flap

Repase y repita
Review and repeat

1 The body

1 **la cabeza**
lah ka<u>be</u>sah

2 **el brazo**
el <u>bra</u>soh

3 **el pecho**
el <u>pe</u>choh

4 **el estómago**
el es<u>to</u>magoh

5 **la pierna**
lah <u>pyair</u>nah

6 **la rodilla**
lah rro<u>dee</u>yah

7 **el pie**
el pee-<u>ay</u>

1 The body

Name the numbered body parts in Spanish.

1 head
2 arm
chest 3
4 stomach
leg 5
knee 6
foot 7

2 On the phone

1 **Quisiera hablar con Ana Flores.**
kee<u>syai</u>rah hab<u>lar</u> kon <u>an</u>na <u>flo</u>res

2 **Luis Cortés de Don Frío.**
<u>loo</u>ees kor<u>tes</u> day don <u>free</u>-oh

3 **¿Puedo dejar un mensaje?**
<u>pwe</u>doh de<u>har</u> oon men<u>sa</u>hay

4 **La cita el lunes a las once está bien.**
lah <u>see</u>tah el <u>loo</u>nes ah las <u>on</u>say es<u>tah</u> byen

5 **Gracias, adiós.**
<u>gra</u>syas, addy-<u>os</u>

2 On the phone

You are arranging an appointment. Follow the conversation, replying in Spanish following the English prompts.

Dígame, Apex Finanzas.
1 *I'd like to speak to Ana Flores.*

¿De parte de quién?
2 *Luis Cortés, of Don Frío.*

Lo siento, la línea está ocupada.
3 *Can I leave a message?*

Sí, dígame.
4 *The appointment on Monday at 11 am is fine.*

Muy bien, adiós.
5 *Thank you, goodbye.*

3 Clothing

Say the Spanish words for the numbered items of clothing.

tie ❶

jacket ❷

pants ❸

❹ *skirt*

shoes ❺   *pantyhose* ❻

3 Clothing

1 **la corbata**
lah kor<u>ba</u>tah

2 **el saco**
el <u>sa</u>koh

3 **el pantalón**
el panta<u>lon</u>

4 **la falda**
lah <u>fal</u>dah

5 **los zapatos**
los sa<u>pa</u>tos

6 **las medias**
las <u>me</u>deeas

4 At the doctor's

Say these phrases in Spanish.

1 *I don't feel well.*

2 *I have a heart condition.*

3 *Do I need to go to the hospital?*

4 *I'm pregnant.*

4 At the doctor's

1 **No me siento
bien.**
noh may <u>syen</u>toh
byen

2 **Tengo un
problema de
corazón.**
<u>ten</u>goh oon
<u>pro</u>blemah day
kora<u>son</u>

3 **¿Necesito ir al
hospital?**
nese<u>see</u>toh eer al
ospee<u>tal</u>

4 **Estoy
embarazada.**
es<u>toy</u>
embara<u>sa</u>dah

1 Warm up

Say the months of the year in Spanish. (pp.28–9)

Ask "Is there parking?" and "Is breakfast included?" (pp.48–9 and pp.58–9)

En casa
At home

Many city-dwellers live in apartment blocks (**edificios**), but in rural areas houses tend to be single-family even if they are small. If you want to know how big a house is, you will need to ask in square meters. If you want to know how many bedrooms there are, ask **¿Cuántos dormitorios hay?**

2 Match and repeat

Match the numbered items to the list and test yourself using the flap.

1 **la chimenea**
lah cheemenayah

2 **la ventana**
lah bentanah

3 **el tejado**
el tehadoh

4 **la terraza**
lah terrasa

5 **la persiana**
lah perseeanah

6 **el muro**
el mooroh

7 **la puerta**
lah pwertah

8 **el garaje**
el garahay

❶ chimney ❷ window

❻ wall

shutters ❺

Cultural tip The second homes of wealthy people often follow the style of Californian or traditional Spanish houses. They will have tiled roofs, window shutters, and even chimneys, though these rarely need to be used. Carpets are not popular; ceramic tiles, stone, wood, or even compressed earth are more common flooring solutions.

3 Words to remember

Familiarize yourself with these words and test yourself using the flap.

¿Cuánto es el alquiler al mes?
kwantoh es el alkeeler al mes
What is the rent per month?

room	**la habitación** lah abeetasyon
floor	**el suelo** el sweloh
ceiling	**el techo** el techoh
bedroom	**el dormitorio** el dormeetoreeoh
bathroom	**el baño** el banyoh
kitchen	**la cocina** lah koseenah
dining room	**el comedor** el komedor
living room	**la sala** lah salah
basement	**el sótano** el sotanoh
attic	**el ático** el ahteekoh

❸ roof

❹ terrace

❽ garage

❼ door

4 Useful phrases

Practice these phrases and test yourself.

¿Hay un garaje?
ah-ee oon garahay

Is there a garage?

¿Cuándo está disponible?
kwandoh estah deesponeeblay

When is it available?

5 Say it

Is there a dining room?

Is it large?

Is it available in July?

¿Está amueblado?
estah amwebladoh

Is it furnished?

What is the Spanish for table, chair, bathroom, and curtains? (pp.20–1, pp.80–1, pp.52–3, pp.60–1)

Say "beautiful," "soft," and "big." (pp.64–5)

En la casa
Inside the house

If you're renting a **casa** (*house*) or a **departamento** (*flat*) long term, you'll be expected to provide a **depósito** (*deposit*) and also a **fiador** (*guarantor*). For short-term rentals, a deposit and personal information are normally sufficient. Check in advance whether the cost of utilities is included.

2 Match and repeat

Match the numbered items to the list in the panel on the left. Then test yourself by concealing the Spanish with the cover flap.

1. la encimera
   lah enseemerah

2. el fregadero
   el fregaderoh

3. el microondas
   el meekro-ondas

4. el horno
   el ornoh

5. la cocina
   lah koseenah

6. el refrigerador
   el rrefreehairador

7. la mesa
   lah mesah

8. la silla
   lah seeyah

❶ *countertop*

❺ *stove*

❻ *refrigerator*

❹ *oven*

table ❼

3 In conversation

Este es el horno.
estay es el ornoh

This is the oven.

¿Hay también un lavavajillas?
ah-ee tambyen oon lababaheeyas

Is there a dishwasher, too?

Sí, y hay un congelador grande.
see, ee ah-ee oon konhelador granday

Yes, and there's a big freezer.

4 Words to remember

Familiarize yourself with these words and test yourself using the flap.

El sofá es nuevo.
el sofah es nweboh
The sofa is new.

wardrobe	**el armario**	el armaryoh
sofa	**el sofá**	el sofah
fireplace	**la chimenea**	lah cheemenayah
carpet	**la alfombra**	lah alfombrah
bathtub	**la tina**	lah teenah
toilet	**la taza**	lah tasah
bathroom sink	**el lavabo**	el lababoh

microwave ❸

❷ *sink*

❽ *chair*

6 Say it

Is there a microwave?

I like the fireplace.

What a soft sofa!

5 Useful phrases

Practice these phrases and then test yourself.

The oven doesn't work.	**El horno no funciona.**	el ornoh noh foonsyonah
I don't like the drapes.	**No me gustan las cortinas.**	noh may goostan las korteenas
Is electricity included?	**¿Está incluida la electricidad?**	estah eenklooeedah lah ehlektreeseedad

Todo está muy nuevo.
todoh estah mwee nweboh

Everything is very new.

Y aquí está la lavadora.
ee ahkee estah lah labadorah

And here's the washing machine.

¡Qué mosaicos tan bonitos!
kay mosaykos tan boneetos

What beautiful tiles!

1 Warm up

Say "I need" and "you need." (pp.64–5, pp.92–4)

What is the Spanish for "day" and "month"? (pp.28–9)

Say the days of the week. (pp.28–9)

El jardín
The backyard

Gardens in Central and South America often display an exuberant profusion of tropical flowers, but need to be watered very frequently outside the rainy season. You will see magnificent bougainvilleas that cover entire walls and flowering poinsettias that can reach a height of 12 feet.

2 Words to remember

Familiarize yourself with these words and test yourself using the flap.

la máquina podadora lah <u>makee</u>nah poda<u>dor</u>ah	*lawnmower*
la horquilla lah or<u>kee</u>yah	*fork*
la pala lah <u>pa</u>lah	*spade*
el rastrillo el rra<u>stree</u>yoh	*rake*
el vivero el bee<u>ber</u>oh	*garden center*

❷ *tree*

❸ *soil*

terrace ❶

flowers ❼   *weeds* ❽   ❾ *path*

3 Useful phrases

Practice these phrases and then test yourself using the cover flap.

	The gardener comes once a week.	**El jardinero viene una vez a la semana.** el hardee_nairoh_ _byainay oonah_ bes ah lah se_manah_
	Can you mow the lawn?	**¿Puede cortar el pasto?** _pwe_day kor_tar_ el _pastoh_
	Is the yard private?	**¿Es privado el jardín?** es pree_badoh_ el har_deen_
	The garden needs watering.	**El jardín necesita que lo rieguen.** el har_deen_ nese_seetah_ kay loh rreeayghen

4 Match and repeat

Match the numbered items to the words in the panel on the right.

④ *lawn* ⑤ *hedge* ⑥ *plants*

flowerbed ⑩

5 Say it

The lawn needs water.

Is there a terrace?

The gardener comes on Fridays.

1 **la terraza**
lah te_rrasah_

2 **el árbol**
el _arbol_

3 **la tierra**
lah _tyairrah_

4 **el pasto**
el _pastoh_

5 **el seto**
el _setoh_

6 **las plantas**
las _plantas_

7 **las flores**
las _flores_

8 **las malas hierbas**
las _malas yerbas_

9 **el camino**
el ka_meenoh_

10 **el arriate**
el a_rryatay_

1 Warm up

Say "My name is …." (pp.8–9)

Say "Don't worry." (pp.94–5)

What's "your" in Spanish? (pp.12–13)

Los animales de compañía
Pets

Avoid touching stray dogs or cats, whether in urban or in rural areas, since they may be infected with rabies (**rabia**). Pets are normally vaccinated once a year, so you needn't worry when visiting people with animals.

2 Match and repeat

Match the numbered animals to the Spanish words in the panel on the left. Then test yourself using the cover flap.

1 **el gato**
el *ga*toh

2 **el conejo**
el ko*ne*hoh

3 **el pájaro**
el *pa*haroh

4 **el pez**
el pes

5 **el perro**
el *pe*rroh

6 **el hámster**
el *ham*ster

bird ❸

❷ *rabbit*

❶ *cat*

fish ❹

dog ❺

❻ *hamster*

3 Useful phrases

Learn these phrases and then test yourself using the cover flap.

¿Es bueno el perro? es *bwe*noh el *pe*rroh	*Is this dog friendly?*
¿Puedo llevar mi perro? *pwe*doh ye*bar* mee *pe*rroh	*Can I bring my dog?*
Me dan miedo los gatos. may dan *myay*doh los *ga*tos	*I'm afraid of cats.*
Mi perro no muerde. mee *pe*rroh noh *mwe*day	*My dog doesn't bite.*

Este gato está lleno de pulgas.
*es*tay *ga*toh es*tah* *ye*noh day *pool*gas
This cat is full of fleas.

Cultural tip Many dogs in Latin America are guard dogs and you may encounter them tethered or roaming free. Approach farms and business premises with particular care. Look out for warning notices such as "¡Cuidado con el perro!" (Beware of the dog).

¡CUIDADO CON EL PERRO!

---

4 Words to remember

Familiarize yourself with these words and test yourself using the flap.

Mi perro no está bien.
mee perroh noh estah byen
My dog is not well.

basket	**la cesta** lah sestah
cage	**la jaula** lah haoolah
bowl	**la cazuela** lah kaswelah
collar	**el collar** el koyar
leash	**la correa** lah korray-ah
vet	**el veterinario** el betereenaryoh
vaccination	**la vacuna** lah bakoonah
flea spray	**el spray antipulgas** el espraee anteepoolgas
muzzle	**el bozal** el bosal

---

5 Put into practice

Join in this conversation. Read the Spanish on the left and follow the instructions to make your reply. Then test yourself by concealing the answers with the cover flap.

¿Es suyo este perro?
es sooyoh estay perroh?
Is this your dog?

Say: Yes, he's called Bosco.

Sí, se llama Bosco.
see, say yamah boskoh

Me dan miedo los perros.
may dan myaydoh los perros
I'm afraid of dogs.

Say: Don't worry. He's friendly.

No se preocupe. Es bueno.
noh say prayohkoopay. es bwenoh

Repase y repita
Review and repeat

1 Colors

1 **negra**
negrah

2 **blancos**
blankos

3 **rojo**
rrohoh

4 **verde**
berday

5 **amarillos**
amareeyos

1 Colors

Complete the sentences with the Spanish for the color in brackets. Be careful to use the correct masculine and feminine form.

1 Quisiera la camisa ____. (black)

2 Me quedo con los zapatos ____. (white)

3 ¿Tiene este traje en ____ ? (red)

4 No, pero lo tengo en ____. (green)

5 Quiero los zapatos ____. (yellow)

2 Kitchen

1 **la cocina**
lah koseenah

2 **el refrigerador**
el rrefreehairador

3 **el fregadero**
el fregaderoh

4 **el microondas**
el meekro-ondas

5 **el horno**
el ornoh

6 **la silla**
lah seeyah

7 **la mesa**
lah mesah

2 Kitchen

Say the Spanish words for the numbered items.

❶ stove

refrigerator ❷

oven ❺

chair ❻

3 House

You want to rent a house. Join in the conversation, asking questions in Spanish following the English prompts.

Ésta es la sala.
1 *What a lovely fireplace.*

Sí, y tiene una cocina muy grande.
2 *How many bedrooms are there?*

Hay tres dormitorios.
3 *Do you have a garage?*

Sí, pero no hay jardín.
4 *When is it available?*

En julio.
5 *What is the rent per month?*

3 House

1 **¡Qué chimenea tan bonita!**
kay cheemenayah tan boneetah

2 **¿Cuántos dormitorios hay?**
kwantos dormeetoreeos ah-ee

3 **¿Tiene garaje?**
tyenay garahay

4 **¿Cuándo está disponible?**
kwandoh estah deesponeeblay

5 **¿Cuánto es el alquiler al mes?**
kwantoh es el alkeeler al mes

microwave **4**

3 *sink*

table **7**

4 At home

Say the Spanish for the following items.

1 *washing machine*

2 *sofa*

3 *attic*

4 *dining room*

5 *tree*

6 *garden*

4 At home

1 **la lavadora**
lah labadorah

2 **el sofá**
el sofah

3 **el ático**
el ahteekoh

4 **el comedor**
el komedor

5 **el árbol**
el arbol

6 **el jardín**
el hardeen

1 Warm up

Ask "How do I get to the bank?" and "How do I get to the post office?" (pp.50–1)

What's the Spanish for "passport"? (pp.54–5)

How do you ask "What time is the meeting?" (pp.30–1)

El banco y la oficina de correos
Bank and post office

Banks usually open only until lunchtime (approximately 2 pm) and are generally closed on weekends. Post offices are open all day, although they might close slightly earlier than the local stores.

2 Words to remember: post

Familiarize yourself with these words and test yourself using the cover flap to conceal the Spanish on the left.

los timbres los <u>teem</u>bres	*stamps*
la postal lah pos<u>tal</u>	*postcard*
el paquete el pa<u>ke</u>tay	*package*
por avión por ab<u>yon</u>	*by air mail*
el correo certificado el ko<u>rra</u>yoh serteefee<u>ka</u>doh	*registered mail*
el buzón el boo<u>son</u>	*mailbox*
el código postal el <u>ko</u>deegoh pos<u>tal</u>	*postal (ZIP) code*
el cartero el kar<u>tai</u>roh	*mail carrier*

¿Cuánto es para el Reino Unido?
<u>kwan</u>toh es <u>pa</u>rah el <u>rray</u>eenoh oo<u>nee</u>doh
How much is it to the United Kingdom?

el sobre el <u>so</u>bray *envelope*

3 In conversation

Quisiera sacar dinero. kee<u>syai</u>rah sa<u>kar</u> dee<u>ne</u>roh

I'd like to withdraw some money.

¿Tiene identificación? <u>tye</u>nay eedenteefeekas<u>yon</u>

Do you have any ID?

Sí, aquí tiene mi pasaporte. see, ah<u>kee</u> <u>tye</u>nay mee pasa<u>por</u>tay

Yes, here's my passport.

4 Words to remember: bank

Familiarize yourself with these words and test yourself using the cover flap to conceal the Spanish on the right.

PIN	**el número personal** el noomairoh personal
bank	**el banco** el bankoh
teller	**el cajero** el kaheroh
ATM	**el cajero automático** el kaheroh aootomateekoh
bills (notes)	**los billetes** los beeyetes
traveler's checks	**los cheques de viajero** los chekes day beeahairoh

¿Cómo puedo pagar?
komoh pwedoh pagar
How can I pay?

5 Useful phrases

Practice these phrases and then test yourself using the flap.

6 Say it

I'd like to change some traveler's checks.

Do I need my passport?

I'd like a stamp for a postcard.

I'd like to change some money.	**Quisiera cambiar dinero.** keesyairah kambyar deeneroh
What is the exchange rate?	**¿A cuánto está el cambio?** ah kwantoh estah el kambyoh
I'd like to withdraw some money.	**Quisiera sacar dinero.** keesyairah sakar deeneroh

Introduzca su número personal, por favor.
introdooskah soo noomairoh personal, por fabor

Please type in your PIN.

¿Tengo que firmar también?
tengoh kay feermar tambyen

Do I have to sign, too?

No, no hace falta.
noh, noh ahsay faltah

No, that's not necessary.

1 Warm up

What is the Spanish for "doesn't work"? (pp.60–1)

What's the Spanish for "today" and "tomorrow"? (pp.28–9)

Los servicios
Services

You can combine the Spanish words on these pages with the vocabulary you learned in week 10 to help you explain basic problems and cope with arranging most repairs. When setting up building work or a repair, it's a good idea to agree on the price and method of payment in advance.

2 Words to remember

Familiarize yourself with these words and test yourself using the flap.

el plomero el plo<u>mai</u>roh	*plumber*
el electricista el ehlektree<u>sees</u>tah	*electrician*
el mecánico el me<u>ka</u>neekoh	*mechanic*
el albañil el alban<u>yeel</u>	*handyman*
la muchacha lah moo<u>cha</u>chah	*cleaner*
el pintor el peen<u>tor</u>	*decorator*
el carpintero el karpeen<u>te</u>roh	*carpenter*
el técnico el <u>tek</u>neekoh	*technician*

la llave de tuercas
lah <u>ya</u>bay day <u>twer</u>kas
tire iron

No necesito un mecánico.
noh nese<u>see</u>toh oon me<u>ka</u>neekoh
I don't need a mechanic.

3 In conversation

La lavadora no funciona.
lah laba<u>do</u>rah noh foonsy<u>o</u>nah

The washing machine's not working.

Sí, la manguera está rota.
see, lah man<u>ghe</u>rah estah <u>rro</u>tah

Yes, the hose is broken.

¿La puede arreglar?
lah <u>pwe</u>day arreglar

Can you repair it?

4 Useful phrases

Practice these phrases and then test yourself using the cover flap.

Can you clean the bathroom?

¿Puede limpiar el baño?
pweday leempyar el banyoh

Can you repair the boiler?

¿Puede arreglar el boiler?
pweday arreglar el boiler

¿Dónde me pueden arreglar la plancha?
donday may pweden arreglar lah planchah
Where can I get the iron repaired?

Do you know a good electrician?

¿Conoce a un buen electricista?
konosay ah oon bwen ehlektreeseestah

5 Put into practice

Join in this conversation. Cover up the text on the right and complete the dialogue in Spanish. Check your answers and repeat if necessary.

los planos
los planos
plans

Empiezo a trabajar mañana.
empyaysoh ah trabahar manyanah
I start work tomorrow.

Su reja está rota.
soo rrehah estah rrotah
Your gate is broken.

Ask: Do you know a good handyman?

¿Conoce a un buen albañil?
konosay ah oon bwen albanyeel

Sí, hay uno en el pueblo.
see ah-ee oonoh en el pwebloh
Yes, there is one in the village.

Ask: Do you have his phone number?

¿Tiene su número de teléfono?
tyenay soo noomeroh day telefonoh

No, va a necesitar una nueva.
noh, bah ah neseseetar oonah nwebah

No, you'll need a new one.

¿Lo puede hacer hoy?
loh pweday ahser oy

Can you do it today?

No, volveré mañana.
noh, bolberay manyanah

No. I'll come back tomorrow.

1 Warm up

Say the days of the week in Spanish. (pp.28–9)

How do you say "cleaner"? (pp.110–11)

Say "It's 9:30," "10:45," "12:00." (pp.30–1)

Venir
To come

The verb **venir** (*to come*) is one of the most useful verbs. As well as the main verb (see below) it is worth knowing the command ¡**ven!**/¡**venga!** (*come here!* informal/formal). Note that *with me* becomes **conmigo** and *with you* **contigo**: **ven conmigo** (*come with me*); **vengo contigo** (*I'm going with you*).

2 Venir: to come

Say the different forms of the verb aloud, reading from the table. Use the cover flap to test yourself and, when you are confident, practice the sample sentences below.

yo vengo yoh <u>ben</u>goh	*I come*
tú vienes/usted viene too <u>bye</u>nes/<u>oos</u>ted <u>bye</u>nay	*you come (informal/formal singular)*
él viene el <u>bye</u>nay	*he comes*
ella viene <u>eh</u>yah <u>bye</u>nay	*she comes*
nosotros/-as venimos no<u>so</u>tros/-as be<u>nee</u>mos	*we come*
ustedes vienen oos<u>te</u>des <u>bye</u>nen	*you come (plural)*
ellos/ellas vienen <u>eh</u>-yos/<u>eh</u>-yas <u>bye</u>nen	*they come*
Vengo ahora. <u>ben</u>goh ah-<u>or</u>ah	*I'm coming now.*
Venimos todos los martes. be<u>nee</u>mos <u>to</u>dos los <u>mar</u>tes	*We come every Tuesday.*
Vienen en tren. <u>bye</u>nen en tren	*They come by train.*

Vienen en muchos colores.
bee<u>ay</u>nen en <u>moo</u>chos ko<u>lo</u>res
They come in many colors.

Conversational tip To say "I come from the US" in Spanish, you use the verb "to be," as in "soy estadounidense" (I am from the US). When you use the verb "to come," as in "Vengo de Nueva York," it means you have just arrived from New York.

3 Useful phrases

Learn these phrases and then test yourself using the cover flap.

When can I come?	**¿Cuándo puedo venir?** kwandoh pwedoh beneer
Does it come in size 44?	**¿Viene en la talla 44?** byenay en lah tayah kwarentah ee kwatroh
The cleaner comes every Monday.	**La muchacha viene todos los lunes.** lah moochachah byenay todos los loones
Come with me. (informal/formal)	**Ven conmigo/ Venga conmigo.** ben konmeegoh/ bengah konmeegoh

¿Puede venir el viernes?
pweday beneer el byernes
Can you come on Friday?

4 Put into practice

Join in this conversation. Cover up the text on the right and say the anwering part of the dialogue in Spanish. Check your answers and repeat if necessary.

Salón de Belleza Marta, dígame. salon day beyesah, deegamay *Marta's Beauty Salon. Can I help you?* *Say: I'd like an appointment.*	**Quisiera una cita.** keesyairah oonah seetah
¿Cuándo quiere venir? kwandoh kyairay beneer *When do you want to come?* *Say: Today, if possible.*	**Hoy, si es posible.** oy, see es poseeblay
Sí, claro. ¿A qué hora? see klaroh, ah kay orah *Yes of course, what time?* *Say: At 10:30.*	**A las diez y media.** ah las dee-es ee medeeah

La policía y el delito
Police and crime

1 Warm up

What's the Spanish for "big" and "small"? (pp.64–5)

Say "The room is big" and "The bed is small." (pp.64–5)

While in Latin America, if you are the victim of a crime, you should go to the police station to report it. You may have to explain your problem in Spanish, at least initially, so some basic vocabulary is useful.

2 Words to remember: crime

Familiarize yourself with these words.

el robo el rroboh	*robbery*
la denuncia lah denoonseeah	*police report*
el ladrón el ladron	*thief*
la policía lah poleeseeah	*police*
la declaración lah deklarasyon	*statement*
el testigo el testeegoh	*witness*
el abogado el abogadoh	*lawyer*

Necesito un abogado.
neseseetoh oon abogadoh
I need a lawyer.

3 Useful phrases

Learn these phrases and then test yourself.

Me han robado. may an rrobadoh	*I've been robbed.*
¿Qué han robado? kay an rrobadoh	*What was stolen?*
¿Vió quién lo hizo? byoh kyain loh eesoh	*Did you see who did it?*
¿Cuándo ocurrió? kwandoh okoorryoh	*When did it happen?*

la cámara fotográfica
lah kamarah fotografeekah
camera

la cartera
la karterah
wallet

4 Words to remember: appearance

Learn these words. Remember, some adjectives have a feminine form.

man	**el hombre**	
	el <u>om</u>bray	
woman	**la mujer**	
	lah moo-<u>hair</u>	
tall	**alto/alta**	
	<u>al</u>toh/<u>al</u>tah	
short	**bajo/baja**	
	<u>ba</u>hoh/<u>ba</u>hah	
young	**joven**	
	<u>ho</u>ben	
old	**viejo/vieja**	
	bee-<u>ay</u>hoh/bee-<u>ay</u>hah	
fat	**gordo/gorda**	
	<u>gor</u>doh/<u>gor</u>dah	
thin	**delgado/delgada**	
	del<u>ga</u>doh/del<u>ga</u>dah	
long/short hair	**el pelo largo/corto**	
	el <u>pe</u>loh <u>lar</u>goh/<u>kor</u>toh	
glasses	**los lentes**	
	los <u>len</u>tes	
beard	**la barba**	
	la <u>bar</u>bah	

Él es bajo y tiene bigote.
el es <u>ba</u>hoh ee <u>tye</u>nay bee<u>go</u>tay
He is short and has a mustache.

Tiene el pelo negro y corto.
<u>tye</u>nay el <u>pe</u>loh <u>ne</u>groh ee <u>kor</u>toh
He has short, black hair.

Cultural tip Police in most of Latin America are called "agentes" (officers), but the organization and uniform varies from country to country. To address a male police officer, you would begin by saying "Disculpe, señor agente."

5 Put into practice

Practice these phrases. Then cover up the text on the right and follow the instructions to make your reply in Spanish.

¿Cómo era?
<u>ko</u>moh <u>eh</u>rah
What did he look like?

Say: Short and fat.

Bajo y gordo.
<u>ba</u>hoh ee <u>gor</u>doh

¿Y el pelo?
ee el <u>pe</u>loh
And his hair?

Say: Long, with a beard.

Largo y con barba.
<u>lar</u>goh ee kon <u>bar</u>bah

Respuestas
Answers
Cover with flap

Repase y repita
Review and repeat

1 To come

1 **vienen**
<u>byen</u>en

2 **viene**
<u>byen</u>ay

3 **venimos**
ben<u>ee</u>mos

4 **vienen**
<u>byen</u>en

5 **vengo**
<u>ben</u>goh

1 To come

Fill in the blanks with the correct form of **venir** (*to come*).

1 Mis padres ___ a las cuatro.

2 La muchacha ___ una vez a la semana.

3 Nosotros ___ todos los martes.

4 ¿ ___ ustedes con nosotros?

5 Yo ___ en taxi.

2 Bank and mail

1 **los billetes**
los bee<u>ye</u>tes

2 **la postal**
la pos<u>tal</u>

3 **el paquete**
el pa<u>ke</u>tay

4 **el sobre**
el <u>so</u>bray

2 Bank and mail

Name the numbered items in Spanish.

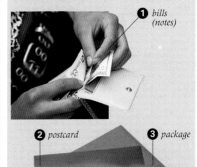

1 *bills (notes)*

2 *postcard*

3 *package*

envelope **4**

3 Appearance

What do these descriptions mean?

1 **Es un hombre alto y delgado.**

2 **Ella tiene el pelo corto y lentes.**

3 **Soy baja y tengo el pelo largo.**

4 **Ella es vieja y gorda.**

5 **Él tiene los ojos azules y barba.**

3 Appearance

1 *He's a tall, thin man.*

2 *She has short hair and glasses.*

3 *I'm short and I have long hair.*

4 *She's old and fat.*

5 *He has blue eyes and a beard.*

4 The pharmacy

You are asking a pharmacist for advice. Join in the conversation, replying in Spanish following the English prompts.

Buenos días, ¿qué desea?
1 *I have a cough.*

¿Le duele el pecho?
2 *No, but I have a headache.*

Tiene estas pastillas.
3 *Do you have that as a syrup?*

Sí también. Aquí tiene.
4 *Thank you. How much is that?*

Veinte pesos.
5 *Here you are. Goodbye.*

4 The pharmacy

1 **Tengo tos.**
tengoh tos

2 **No, pero me duele la cabeza.**
noh, peroh may dwelay lah kabesah

3 **¿Lo tiene en jarabe?**
loh tyenay en harabay

4 **Gracias. ¿Cuánto es?**
grasyas. kwantoh es

5 **Aquí tiene. Adiós.**
ahkee tyenay. addy-os

1 Warm up

What is the Spanish for "museum" and "art gallery"? (pp.48–9)

Say "I don't like the curtains." (pp.100–1)

Ask "Do you want…?" informally. (pp.24–5)

El ocio
Leisure time

Music and dancing feature strongly in the popular culture of Latin America. Each Spanish-speaking country has its own regional dance, with the most famous being the Cuban Salsa. In Mexico, many people also enjoy dancing to the music of the traditional **mariachis** bands.

Me encanta el baile.
me enkantah el baeelay
I love dancing.

2 Words to remember

Familiarize yourself with these words and test yourself using the cover flap to conceal the Spanish on the left.

el teatro el te-ahtroh	*theater*
el cine el seenay	*movie theater*
la discoteca lah deeskotekah	*discotheque*
el deporte el deportay	*sports*
el turismo el tooreesmoh	*sightseeing*
la política la poleeteekah	*politics*
la música lah mooseekah	*music*
el arte el artay	*art*

3 In conversation

Hola. ¿Quieres jugar al tenis hoy?
olah. kyaires hoogar al tenis oy

Hi. Do you want to play tennis today?

No, no me gusta el deporte.
noh, noh may goostah el deportay

No, I don't like sports.

Y entonces, ¿qué te gusta?
ee entonses, kay tay goostah

So, what do you like?

4 Useful phrases

Learn these phrases and then test yourself using the cover flap.

los video-juegos
los <u>bee</u>dayoh-<u>hwe</u>gos
video games

el traje típico
el <u>tra</u>hay <u>tee</u>peekoh
traditional costume

What are your (formal/informal) interests?	**¿Cuáles son sus/tus intereses?** <u>kwa</u>les son soos/toos inte<u>re</u>ses
I like the theater.	**Me gusta el teatro.** me <u>goos</u>tah el te-<u>ah</u>troh
I prefer the movies.	**Yo prefiero el cine.** yoh pref<u>yai</u>roh el <u>see</u>nay
I'm interested in art.	**Me interesa el arte.** may inte<u>re</u>sah el <u>ar</u>tay
That bores me.	**Eso me aburre.** <u>eh</u>soh may a<u>boo</u>rray

la bailadora
lah baeela<u>do</u>rah
dancer

5 Say it

I'm interested in music.

I prefer sports.

I don't like video games.

Prefiero ir de compras.
pref<u>yai</u>roh eer day <u>kom</u>pras

I prefer shopping.

Eso a mí no me interesa.
<u>eh</u>soh ah mee noh may inte<u>re</u>sah

That doesn't interest me.

No importa. Me voy yo sola.
noh im<u>por</u>tah. may boy yoh <u>so</u>lah

No problem. I'll go on my own.

1 Warm up

Ask "Do you (formal)
want to play tennis?"
(pp.118–19)

Say "I like the
theater" and "I prefer
sightseeing."
(pp.118–19)

Say "That doesn't
interest me."
(pp.118–19)

El deporte y los pasatiempos
Sports and hobbies

Hacer (*to do* or *to make*) and **jugar** (*to play*) are the verbs used most when talking about sports and pastimes. **Jugar** is followed by **a** when you are talking about playing a sport, as in **juego al baloncesto** (*I play basketball*).

2 Words to remember

Familiarize yourself with these words and then test yourself.

el futbol/rugby el foot<u>bol</u>/<u>roog</u>bee	*soccer/rugby*
el tenis/baloncesto el <u>ten</u>is/balon<u>ses</u>toh	*tennis/basketball*
la natación lah natas<u>yon</u>	*swimming*
la vela lah <u>be</u>lah	*sailing*
la pesca lah <u>pes</u>kah	*fishing*
la pintura lah peen<u>too</u>rah	*painting*
el ciclismo el seek<u>lees</u>moh	*cycling*
el excursionismo el exkoorsyo<u>nees</u>moh	*hiking*

el bunker
el <u>bun</u>ker
bunker

el jugador de golf
el <u>hu</u>gador day golf
golfer

Juego al golf todos los días.
<u>hwe</u>goh al golf todos los <u>dee</u>yas
I play golf every day.

3 Useful phrases

Learn these phrases and then test yourself.

Juego al futbol. <u>hwe</u>goh al foot<u>bol</u>	*I play soccer.*
Juega al tenis. <u>hwe</u>gah al <u>ten</u>is	*He plays tennis.*
Ella pinta. <u>eh</u>-yah <u>peen</u>tah	*She paints.*

4 Hacer: to do or to make

Hacer is a useful verb meaning "to do" or "to make." It is commonly used to describe leisure pursuits. **Hace** is also used to describe the weather.

Hoy hace buen tiempo.
oy <u>ah</u>say bwen <u>tyem</u>poh
It's nice out today.

la banderola
lah bandai<u>ro</u>lah
flag

**el campo
de golf**
el <u>kam</u>poh
day golf
golf course

I do	**yo hago** yoh <u>ah</u>goh
you do (informal)	**tú haces** too <u>ah</u>ses
you do (formal singular)	**usted hace** oos<u>ted</u> ah<u>say</u>
he/she does	**él/ella hace** el/<u>eh</u>-yah ah<u>say</u>
we do	**nosotros/-as hacemos** no<u>so</u>tros/-as ah<u>se</u>mos
you do (plural)	**ustedes hacen** oos<u>te</u>des <u>ah</u>sen
they do	**ellos/ellas hacen** <u>eh</u>-yos/<u>eh</u>-yas <u>ah</u>sen
What do you like doing? (informal/formal)	**¿Qué te/le gusta hacer?** kay tay/lay <u>goos</u>tah ah<u>sair</u>?
I go hiking.	**Hago excursionismo.** <u>ah</u>goh exkoorsyo<u>nees</u>moh

5 Put into practice

Join in this conversation following the English prompts.

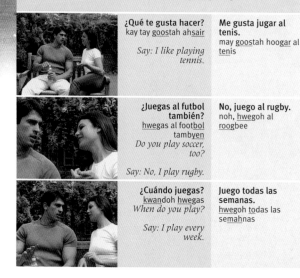

¿Qué te gusta hacer?
kay tay <u>goos</u>tah ah<u>sair</u>

Say: I like playing tennis.

Me gusta jugar al tenis.
may <u>goos</u>tah hoo<u>gar</u> al <u>ten</u>is

¿Juegas al futbol también?
<u>hwe</u>gas al foot<u>bol</u> tamb<u>yen</u>
Do you play soccer, too?

Say: No, I play rugby.

No, juego al rugby.
noh, <u>hwe</u>goh al <u>roog</u>bee

¿Cuándo juegas?
<u>kwan</u>doh <u>hwe</u>gas
When do you play?

Say: I play every week.

Juego todas las semanas.
<u>hwe</u>goh <u>to</u>das las se<u>mah</u>nas

1 Warm up

Say "my husband"
and "my wife."
(pp.10–11)

Say the days of the
week in Spanish.
(pp.28–9)

Say "Sorry, I'm busy."
(pp.32–3)

La vida social
Socializing

Throughout Latin America, a major
leisure pusuit is having a relaxed meal
with friends or family. This will often
merge into a **sobremesa** (after-dinner
conversation). It is not good manners
to arrive at someone´s house exactly
on time. You should allow a few
minutes' grace.

2 Useful phrases

Practice these phrases and then test yourself.

Me gustaría invitarte a cenar. may goostar<u>ee</u>ah inbeet<u>ar</u>tay ah se<u>nar</u>	*I'd like to invite you to dinner.*
¿Estás libre el miércoles que viene? est<u>as</u> <u>lee</u>bray el my<u>air</u>koles kay <u>byen</u>ay	*Are you free next Wednesday?*
Quizá otro día. kees<u>ah</u> <u>ohtroh</u> <u>dee</u>yah	*Maybe another day.*

Cultural tip When you visit someone's house for
the first time, it is better to bring flowers than wine. If
you are invited again, having seen your host's house,
you can bring something a little more personal.

3 In conversation

¿Quieres venir a comer el martes?
<u>kyaires</u> be<u>neer</u> ah ko<u>mer</u> el <u>martes</u>

Would you like to come to lunch on Tuesday?

Lo siento, estoy ocupada.
loh s<u>yain</u>toh, es<u>toy</u> okoo<u>pa</u>dah

I'm sorry, I'm busy.

¿Qué tal el jueves?
kay tal el <u>hwe</u>bes

What about Thursday?

4 Words to remember

Familiarize yourself with these words and test yourself using the flap.

la anfitriona
lah anfeetr<u>yo</u>nah
hostess

    la invitada
    lah inbeet<u>a</u>dah
      guest

party	**la fiesta** lah f<u>yay</u>stah
dinner party	**la cena** lah <u>se</u>nah
invitation	**la invitación** lah inbeetas<u>yon</u>
reception	**la recepción** lah rreseps<u>yon</u>
cocktail party	**el coctel** el kok<u>tel</u>

5 Put into practice

Join in this conversation.

**¿Puede venir a una
recepción esta
noche?**
p<u>we</u>day ben<u>eer</u> ah
<u>oo</u>nah rreseps<u>yon</u>
<u>e</u>stah <u>no</u>chay
*Can you come to a
reception tonight?*

Say: Yes, I'd love to.

Sí, encantado/-a.
see, enkan-<u>ta</u>doh/-ah

Empieza a las ocho.
emp<u>yay</u>sah ah las
<u>o</u>choh
*It starts at eight
o'clock.*

*Ask: What should I
wear?*

¿Qué me pongo?
kay may <u>pon</u>goh

Gracias por invitarnos.
<u>gra</u>syas por inbeet<u>ar</u>nos
*Thank you for
inviting us.*

Encantada.
enkan-<u>ta</u>dah

I'd love to.

Ven con tu marido.
ben kon too mar<u>ee</u>doh

*Come with your
husband.*

Gracias. ¿A qué hora?
<u>gra</u>syas, ah kay <u>o</u>rah

*Thank you. What
time?*

Repase y repita
Review and repeat

1 Animals

1 **el pez**
el pes

2 **el pájaro**
el paharoh

3 **el conejo**
el konehoh

4 **el gato**
el gatoh

5 **el hámster**
el hamster

6 **el perro**
el perroh

1 Animals

Name the animals.

1 fish

2 bird

4 cat

5 hamster

2 I like...

1 **Me gusta el futbol.**
may goostah el footbol

2 **No me gusta el golf.**
noh may goostah el golf

3 **Me gusta la pintura.**
may goostah lah peentoorah

4 **No me gustan las flores.**
noh may goostan las flores

2 I like...

Say the following in Spanish:

1 *I like soccer.*

2 *I don't like golf.*

3 *I like painting.*

4 *I don't like flowers.*

❸ *rabbit*

❻ *dog*

❸ Hacer

Use the correct form of the verb **hacer** (*to do* or *make*) in these sentences.

1 Ustedes ____ senderismo?

2 Ella ____ eso todos los días.

3 ¿Qué ____ tú?

4 Hoy no ____ frío.

5 ¿Qué ____ ellos esta noche?

6 Yo ____ natación.

❸ Hacer

1 **hacen**
   <u>ah</u>sen

2 **hace**
   <u>ah</u>say

3 **haces**
   <u>ah</u>ses

4 **hace**
   <u>ah</u>say

5 **hacen**
   <u>ah</u>sen

6 **hago**
   <u>ah</u>goh

❹ An invitation

You are invited for dinner. Join in the conversation, replying in Spanish following the English prompts.

   ¿Quieres venir a comer el viernes?
1 *I'm sorry, I'm busy.*

   ¿Qué tal el sábado?
2 *I'd love to.*

   Ven con los niños.
3 *Thank you. What time?*

   A las doce y media.
4 *That's good for me.*

❹ An invitation

1 **Lo siento, estoy ocupado/-a.**
   loh <u>syen</u>toh, es<u>toy</u> okoo<u>pa</u>doh/-ah

2 **Encantado/-a.**
   enkan-<u>ta</u>doh/-ah

3 **Gracias. ¿A qué hora?**
   <u>gra</u>syas. ah kay <u>o</u>rah

4 **Me viene bien.**
   may <u>bye</u>nay byen

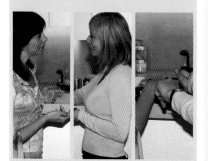

Reinforce and progress

Regular practice is the key to maintaining and advancing your language skills. In this section you will find a variety of suggestions for reinforcing and extending your knowledge of Latin American Spanish. Many involve returning to exercises in the book and using the dictionaries to extend their scope. Go back through the lessons in a different order, mix and match activities to make up your own 15-minute daily program, or focus on topics that are of particular relevance to your current needs.

Keep warmed up

Revisit the Warm Up boxes to remind yourself of key words and phrases. Make sure you work your way through all of them on a regular basis.

1 Warm up

Say "I'm sorry."
(pp.32–3)

What is the Spanish for "I'd like an appointment"?
(pp.22–3 and pp.32–3)

How do you say "when?" in Spanish?
(pp.32–3)

2 I'd like...

Say "I'd like" the following:

churros **2**   sugar **3**

1 black coffee

coffee with **4** milk

Review and repeat again

Work through a Review and Repeat lesson as a way of reinforcing words and phrases presented in the course. Return to the main lesson for any topic on which you are no longer confident.

3 In conversation: taxi

Carry on conversing
Reread the In Conversation panels. Say both parts of the conversation, paying attention to the pronunciation. Where possible, try incorporating new words from the dictionary.

Al Parque España, por favor.
al parkay espanyah, por fabor

To España Park, please.

Sí, de acuerdo, señor.
see, day akwairdo, senyor

Yes, certainly, sir.

¿Me puede dejar aqu por favor?
may pweday dehar ahkee, por fabor

Can you drop me her please?

4 Useful phrases

Learn these phrases and then test yourself using the cover flap.

ABIERTO OPEN	What time do you open/close?	¿A qué hora abre/cierra? ah kay orah ahbray/syairrah
	Where are the restrooms?	¿Dónde están los baños? donday estan los banyos
	Is there access for wheelchairs?	¿Hay acceso para sillas de ruedas? ah-ee aksesoh parah seeyas day rwedas

Practice phrases
Return to the Useful Phrases and Put into Practice exercises. Test yourself using the cover flap. When you are confident, devise your own versions of the phrases, using new words from the dictionary.

Match, repeat, and extend

Remind yourself of words related to specific topics by returning to the Match and Repeat and Words to Remember exercises. Test yourself using the cover flap. Discover new words in that area by referring to the dictionary and menu guide.

5 Match and repeat

Match the numbered items in this scene with the text in the panel.

1 **los jitomates**
los heetomates

2 **los ejotes**
los ehotes

3 **los hongos**
los ongos

4 **las uvas**
las oobas

5 **los pepinos**
los pepeenos

6 **las alcachofas**
las alkachofas

7 **los chícharos**
los cheecharos

8 **los pimientos**
los peemyaintos

2 *beans*
3 *mushrooms*
4 *grapes*
1 *tomatoes*
5 *cucumbers*
peas 7
artichokes 6
peppers 8

Say it again
The Say It exercises are a useful instant reminder for each lesson. Practice these, using your own vocabulary variations from the dictionary or elsewhere in the lesson.

6 Say it
The lawn needs watering.
Are there any trees?
The gardener comes on Fridays.

Using other resources

In addition to working with this book, try the following language extension ideas:

- Visit a Spanish-speaking country and try out your new skills. Find out if there is a Spanish-speaking community near you. There may be shops, cafés, restaurants, and clubs. Try to visit some of these and use your Spanish to order food and drink and strike up conversations. Most native speakers will be happy to speak Spanish to you.

- Join a language class or club. There are usually evening and day classes available at a variety of different levels. Or you could start a club yourself if you have friends who are also interested in keeping up their Spanish.

- Look at Spanish-language magazines and newspapers. Advertisements are also a useful way of expanding your vocabulary.

- Use the Internet, where you can find all kinds of websites for learning languages, some of which offer free online help and activities. You can also find Latin American websites for everything from renting a house to cooking. You can even access Latin American radio and TV stations online. Start by going to a Latin American search engine, such as *latinworld.com*, and keying in a subject that interests you, or set yourself a challenge, such as finding an apartment for rent in Buenos Aires.

Menu guide

This guide lists the most common terms you may encounter on menus or when shopping for food. If you can't find an exact phrase, try looking up its component parts.

A

aceitunas *olives*
acelgas *chard*
achicoria *chicory*
aguacate *avocado*
ahumados *smoked fish*
aji *chili*
ajiaco *stew of chicken, potatoes, vegetables, and corn on the cob*
ajo *garlic*
a la parrilla *grilled*
a la plancha *grilled*
a la romana *in batter*
albaricoques *apricots*
albóndigas *meatballs*
alcachofas *artichokes*
alcaparras *capers*
al horno *baked*
almejas *clams*
almendras *almonds*
alubias *beans*
anchoas *anchovies*
anguila *eel*
angulas *baby eels*
anticuchos *beef kebabs*
arenque *herring*
arepa *cornmeal pancake*
aromáticas *herb teas*
arroz a la cubana *rice with fried eggs*
arroz a la valenciana *rice with seafood*
arroz con leche *rice pudding*
arroz moro *rice with spiced meat*
arvejas *peas*
asado *roast*
asado de tira *spare ribs*
atún *tuna*
avellanas *hazelnuts*
azúcar *sugar*

B

bacalao a la vizcaína *cod with ham, peppers, and garlic*
bacalao al pil pil *cod with chili pepper and garlic*
baleada *cornmeal pancake filled with beans, cheese, and eggs*
bandeja paisa *beef, beans, eggs, rice, and vegetables*
batido *milkshake*

berenjena *eggplant*
besugo *sea bream*
bife *steak*
bistec de ternera *veal steak*
bizcochos *sponge cakes*
blanquillos *eggs*
bolillo *bread roll*
bonito *fish similar to tuna*
boquerones *fresh anchovies*
borracho *cake soaked in rum*
brazo de gitano *sponge cake with jam filling*
broqueta de riñones *kidney kebabs*
budín *cake*
budín inglés *trifle*
buñuelos *light fried pastries; doughnuts*
burritos *burritos with sauce*
buseca *oxtail soup with peas and beans*
butifarra *spicy blood sausage*

C

cabrito *kid*
cachelada *pork stew with tomatoes, onion, and garlic*
cachito *croissant or baked bread roll with savory filling (Venezuela)*
café americano *weak black coffee (Mexico)*
café cortado *coffee with a dash of milk*
café de olla *coffee made with cinammon and raw sugar*
café perfumado *coffee with a dash of brandy or other spirits*
café perico *coffee with a dash of milk*
café solo *black coffee*
café tinto *black coffee (Colombia)*
caguama *turtle*
calabacín/calabacita *zucchini*
calabaza *pumpkin*
calamares *squid*
calamares a la romana *squid rings in batter*

calamares en su tinta *squid cooked in their ink*
caldeirada *fish soup*
caldereta gallega *vegetable stew*
caldo *soup*
caldo de pescado *clear fish soup*
caldo gallego *vegetable soup*
caldo guanche *potato soup*
callampas *mushrooms (Chile)*
callos a la madrileña *tripe with chili peppers*
camarones *baby shrimp*
camote *sweet potato*
cangrejos de río *river crabs*
caracoles *snails*
caramelos *candy*
caraotas *beans*
carne de chancho/cerdo *pork*
carne de res *beef*
carnes *meat, meat dishes*
carnitas *barbecued pork*
carro de queso *cheese board*
castañas *chestnuts*
cazuela *stew*
cebolla *onion*
cebollines *green onions*
cecina *corned beef*
centollo *spider crab*
cerdo *pork*
cerezas *cherries*
cerveza *beer*
ceviche *marinated raw seafood cocktail*
chairo *mutton and potato broth*
champiñones *mushrooms*
chancho *pork*
chanquetes *fish similar to whitebait*
chauchas *green beans*
chayote *vegetable similar to squash*
chícharos *peas*
chicharrón *pork cracklings*
chile *chili pepper*
chile poblano *green pepper (Mexico)*
chiles rellenos *stuffed peppers*
chipirones *baby squid*
chipotle *dark chili sauce*

crentimoya *green heart-shaped fruit*

crentmol *hot sauce made from tomatoes, onion, and mint*

choclo *corn*

chocolate santafereño *hot chocolate and cheese (Bolivia)*

chocos *squid*

cholgas *mussels*

chongos *pot cheese in sweet syrup*

chop *beer (Chile)*

chuleta *chop (cutlet)*

chuletón *large chop (cutlet)*

chuños *freeze-dried potatoes (Peru, Bolivia)*

churisco *baked sausage*

churrasco *roast and grilled meats*

churros *deep-fried pastry sticks*

cigalas *crayfish*

cilantro *coriander*

ciruelas *plums*

ciruelas pasas *prunes*

clérico *wine, fruit, and fruit juice*

cochinillo *suckling pig*

cocido *stew of meat, chickpeas, or chicken*

coco *coconut*

cóctel de mariscos *seafood cocktail*

codornices *quail*

col *cabbage*

coliflor *cauliflower*

completo *hot dog*

conejo *rabbit*

congrio *conger eel*

copa de helado *assorted ice cream*

cordero *lamb*

cordero chillindrón *lamb stew*

costillas de cerdo *pork ribs*

cotufa *Jerusalem artichoke*

crema catalana *crème brûlée*

cremada *dessert made with eggs and butter*

crema de espárragos *cream of asparagus soup*

crepa *sweet crepe*

criadillas *bull's testicles*

criadillas de tierra *truffles*

crocante *ice cream with chopped nuts*

croquetas *croquettes*

cuajada *milk curds*

cuitlacoche *type of edible mushroom*

culantro *coriander*

curanto *dish of various meats, seafood, and vegetables (Chile)*

cusuco *armadillo*

cuy *guinea pig*

D, E

damasco *apricot*

dátiles *dates*

dulce *sugar*

durazno *peach*

ejotes *runner beans*

elote *corn, corn on the cob*

embutidos *sausages, cold meats*

empanada *pastry filled with meat, cheese, or fish*

empanada santiaguesa *fish pie*

empanadillas *pasties*

enchilada *fried cornmeal pancake filled with meat, vegetables, or cheese in sauce*

endivias *chicory*

ensalada *salad*

escarola *curly endive*

espada *swordfish*

espaguetis *spaghetti*

espárragos *asparagus*

espinacas *spinach*

espinacas a la crema *creamed spinach*

espinazo de cerdo con patatas *stew of pork ribs with potatoes*

estofado *stew*

estragón *tarragon*

F

fabada (asturiana) *bean stew with sausage*

faisán *pheasant*

fiambres *cold meats*

fideos *thin noodles*

filete a la parrilla *grilled beef*

flan *crème caramel*

flauta *cornmeal pancake, filled with chicken*

flor de calabaza *pumpkin flower*

frambuesas *raspberries*

fresas *strawberries*

fresco *fruit juice (Central America)*

fresones *strawberries*

frijoles *kidney beans*

frijoles refritos *refried beans*

fritada *pieces of fried meat*

frito *fried*

fritos con jamón *fried eggs with ham*

fruta *fruit*

fruta bomba *papaya (Cuba)*

frutas en almíbar *fruit in syrup*

frutillas *strawberries*

G

gallina *chicken*

gallina en pepitoria *chicken stewed with peppers*

gallo pinto *rice and beans (Central America)*

gallos *cornmeal pancakes filled with meat or chicken in sauce*

gambas *shrimp*

gambas a la americana *shrimp*

gambas en gabardina *shrimp in batter*

gambas rebozadas *shrimp in batter*

garbanzos *chickpeas*

garbanzos a la catalana *chickpeas with sausage, boiled eggs, and pine nuts*

garobo *iguana*

gazpacho andaluz *cold tomato soup*

gelatina *gelatin*

gorditas *thick fried pancake with sauce*

gratén de... *baked in a cream and cheese sauce*

grelo *turnip*

guacamole *avocado dip*

guanábana *green heart-shaped fruit*

guayaba *guava*

guineo *small banana*

guisantes *peas*

H

habas *broad beans*

habichuelas *beans*

helado *ice cream*

helado de turrón *nougat ice cream*

hígado *liver*

hongos *mushrooms*

hormigas culonas *large fried ants*

huachinango *red snapper*

huevo hilado *egg yolk garnish*

huevos *eggs*

huevos a la flamenca *fried eggs with ham and tomato*

huevos a la mexicana *eggs with peppers, onions, and garlic*

huevos cocidos *hard-boiled eggs*

huevos duros *hard-boiled eggs*

huevos escalfados *poached eggs*

huevos pasados por agua *soft-boiled eggs*

huevos pericos *scrambled eggs with tomato and onion*

huevos rancheros *fried eggs with spicy tomato sauce*
huevos revueltos *scrambled eggs*
humitas *sweet corn tamales*
húngaro *hot dog with spicy sausage in a white sauce*

J

jaiba *crab*
jalapeños *hot green chili peppers*
jamón *ham*
jamón serrano *dry-cured ham*
jeta *pigs' cheeks*
jícama *sweet turniplike fruit*
jitomate *tomato*
judías verdes *green beans*
jugo *fruit juice*

L

langosta *lobster*
langosta a la americana *lobster with brandy and garlic*
langostinos *jumbo shrimp*
leche *milk*
leche frita *semolina pudding with milk and eggs*
leche merengada *cold milk with meringues*
lechona *suckling pig*
lechosa *papaya*
lechuga *lettuce*
lengua de buey *ox tongue*
lengua de cordero estofada *stewed lambs' tongue*
lenguado a la parrilla *grilled sole*
lenguado a la romana *sole in batter*
lentejas *lentils*
lima *lemon, lime*
limón *lemon*
llapingachos *potato and cheese crepes*
locro *corn and meat soup*
lombarda *red cabbage*
lomo *pork fillet*
lomo curado *pork-loin sausage*
longaniza *spicy sausage*
lubina *sea bass*

M

macarrones gratinados *macaroni and cheese*
macho *large green banana*
maíz *corn*
mamey *round, apple-sized tropical fruit*
maní/manises *peanuts*
manitas de cordero *lamb shank*
manos de cerdo *pigs' feet*
manteca *butter (Argentina, Uruguay)*
mantecadas *small sponge cakes*
mantequilla *butter*
manzanas *apples*
maracuyá *passion fruit*
mariscada *cold mixed shellfish*
mariscos *shellfish*
masa *dough*
matambre arrollado *rolled beef stuffed with spinach, onion, carrots, and eggs*
mate *bitter tea*
mazápan *marzipan*
mejillones *mussels*
melocotón *peach*
melocotones en almíbar *peaches in syrup*
membrillo *quince jelly*
menestra de legumbres *vegetable stew*
merengada *fruit juice with ice, milk, and sugar*
merluza *grilled hake*
mermelada *jam*
mero *grouper*
milanesa *breaded chop or scallop*
mole *thick dark chili sauce, or dessert made from banana and chocolate (Guatemala)*
mollejas de ternera *sweetbreads*
mondongo *tripe*
mora *blackberry*
morros de cerdo *pigs' cheeks*
morros de vaca *cows' cheeks*
morteruelo *type of mince pie*
mosh *oats with cinnamon and honey (Guatemala)*

N

nabo *turnip*
nacatamales *cornmeal dough filled with meat in sauce and steamed in banana leaves*
naranjas *oranges*
natillas *cold custard*
níscalos *wild mushrooms*
nixtamal *cornmeal dough*
nopalitos *pickled chopped cactus leaves*
nueces *walnuts*

O, P

ostras *oysters*
pabellón *ground meat, beans, rice, and banana (Venezuela)*
pachamanca *meat cooked in clay (Peru)*
pacumutu *beef kebabs*
paella *fried rice with various meats*
paella valenciana *fried rice with shellfish and chicken*
paila *fried or poached eggs with bread*
paleta de cordero lechal *shoulder of lamb*
palta *avocado*
pan *bread*
pana *liver (Chile)*
panceta *bacon*
pancita *tripe*
pan de higos *dried fig cake with cinnamon*
pan dulce *buns and cakes*
papa *potato*
papas a la criolla *potatoes in hot, spicy sauce*
papas a la huancaína *stuffed potato (Per)*
papas bravas *potatoes with spicy tomato sauce*
parchita *passion fruit*
pargo *fish*
parrillada de caza *mixed grilled game*
parrillada de mariscos *mixed grilled shellfish*
pasas *raisins*
pastel de ternera *veal pie*
pasteles *cakes*
pasticho *lasagna (Venezuela)*
patacón *mashed potato and banana (Colombia)*
patatas *chips*
patín *tomato-based sauce*
pato *duck*
pavipollo *large chicken*
pavo *turkey*
pepián *meat stew*
pepinillos *pickles*
pepino *cucumber*
peras *pears*
percebes *edible barnacles*
perdices *partridges*
perejil *parsley*
pescado *fish*
pestiños *sugared pastries*
píbil *dark sauce*
picadillo *ground meat*
picante/picoso *hot, spicy*
pichón *pigeon*
piloncillo *raw sugar*
pimienta *black pepper*
pimientos *peppers*
pimientos morrones *strong peppers*
pinchitos *bar snacks*

pincho *kebab*
piña *pineapple*
piñones *pine nuts*
pipián *hot chili sauce*
pique macho *chopped beef with onions*
pisto *fried mixed vegetables*
pisto manchego *squash with onion and tomato*
pitahaya *red fruit of a cactus plant with soft, sweet flesh*
plátanos *bananas*
plato montañero *beef, sausage, beans, eggs, and rice*
poblano *green pepper (Mexico)*
pollo *chicken*
pollo en cacerola *chicken casserole*
pollo en pepitoria *chicken in wine with saffron, garlic, and almonds*
polvorones *sugar-based dessert*
pomelo *grapefruit*
porotos *kidney beans*
potaje *thick broth*
pozole *corn and meat stew*
puchero canario *meat casserole with chickpeas*
puerco chuk *pork stew*
pulpo *octopus*
pupusa *dumpling usually filled with cheese or meat (Central America)*
purrusalda *cod with leeks and potatoes*

Q, R

queque *cake*
quesadilla *fried cornmeal crepe*
queso *cheese*
queso de cabra *goat's cheese*
queso de oveja *sheep cheese*
quisquillas *shrimp*
rajas *grilled green peppers*
rape a la cazuela *stewed monkfish*
raya *skate*
rebozado *in batter*
redondo al horno *roast fillet of beef*
refresco *soft drink, carbonated drink*
refritos *refried beans*
relleno *stuffed*
remolacha *beet*
repollo *cabbage*
requesón *cream cheese, cottage cheese*
res *beef*
riñones *kidneys*

róbalo *bass*
rocoto *hot red pepper*
rodaballo *turbot*
romero *rosemary*
ropa vieja *shredded meat*
rosca *traditional sponge cake*
roscas *sweet pastries*

S, T

saice/saisi *spicy meat broth (Bolivia)*
sajta *chicken in hot sauce (Bolivia)*
sal *salt*
salchichas *sausages*
salchichón *white sausage with pepper*
salmón *salmon*
salmonetes *red mullet*
salmorejo *thick sauce made with bread*
salpicón de mariscos *shellfish with vinaigrette*
salsa *sauce*
salsa ali oli/allioli *mayonnaise with garlic*
salsa tártara *tartar sauce*
salsa verde *hot sauce with chili pepper and tomatoes*
salteado *sautéed*
salteño *small pie usually filled with chicken or other meat and sauce*
sancocho *vegetable soup with meat or fish*
sandía *watermelon*
sardinas *sardines*
seco *dry; main dish; stew*
semidulce *medium-sweet*
sesos *brains*
setas *mushrooms*
silpancho *beef with eggs (Bolivia)*
sobreasada *soft red sausage with cayenne*
solomillo con patatas *fillet steak with chips*
solomillo frio *cold roast beef*
sopa *soup*
sopa de fideos *noodle soup*
sopa mallorquina *soup with tomatoes and meat*
sopa seca *rice course*
sopa sevillana *fish and mayonnaise soup*
sorbete *sorbet*
surubí *a freshwater fish*
taco *taco*
tajadas *fried banana strips*
tallarines *noodles*
tallarines a la italiana *tagliatelle*
tamales *cornmeal dough filled with meat and*

sauce then steamed in banana or corn leaves
tamarindo *tamarind*
tapado *stew*
tarta de almendra *rich almond cake*
tarta de chocolate *rich chocolate cake*
tarta de fresas *strawberry tart or cake*
tarta de manzana *apple tart*
tarta helada *rich ice-cream cake*
tarta moca *mocha tart*
ternera *veal*
tocino *bacon*
tomates rellenos *stuffed tomatoes*
tomillo *thyme*
tordo *thrush*
toronja *grapefruit*
torrejas *French toast*
torrijas *sweet pastries*
torta *cake, pie; filled roll (Mexico)*
tortilla *tortilla*
tortilla de harina *wheat-flour tortilla*
tortilla de huevo *omelet*
tostadas *fried crisp tortilla with sauce*
trucha *trout*
trucha ahumada *smoked trout*
truchas molinera *trout meunière (trout dipped in flour, fried and served with butter, lemon juice, and parsley)*
tuna *prickly pear*
tuntas *freeze-dried potatoes (Guatemala)*
turrón *nougat*
turrón de Jijona *soft nougat*

U, V

uvas *grapes*
vainitas *green beans*
vieiras *scallops*
vino blanco *white wine*
vino rosado *rosé wine*
vino tinto *red wine*
vuelvealavida *marinated seafood cocktail with chili pepper*

Y, Z

yaguarlocro *potato soup with sausage*
yerba mate *herbal tea*
yuca *cassava*
zanahorias *carrots*
zapallo *quash*
zapote *sweet pumpkin*
zarzamoras *blackberries*
zarzuela de mariscos *seafood stew*

Dictionary
English to Spanish

The gender of a Spanish noun is indicated by the word for *the*: **el** and **la** (masculine and feminine singular) or their plural forms **los** (masculine) and **las** (feminine). Spanish adjectives (adj) vary according to the gender and number of the word they describe; the masculine form is shown here. In general, adjectives that end in "o" adopt an "a" ending in the feminine form, and those that end in "e" usually stay the same. For the plural, an "s" is added. Some words are used only in certain Latin American countries or regions, which are indicated by the following abbreviations:

(Arg)	Argentina	(ElS)	El Salvador
(Bol)	Bolivia	(Gua)	Guatemala
(CAm)	Central America	(Mex)	Mexico
(Chi)	Chile	(Nic)	Nicaragua
(Col)	Colombia	(Per)	Peru
(Cos)	Costa Rica	(Uru)	Uruguay
(Cub)	Cuba	(Ven)	Venezuela

A

a un/una
able: to be able to poder
about: about 16 alrededor de dieciséis
accelerator el acelerador
accident el accidente
accommodation el alojamiento
accountant el/la contador
ache el dolor
across from: across from the hotel frente al hotel
adapter el adaptador
address la dirección
admission charge el precio de entrada
airplane el avión
after ... después de ...
aftershave el after-shave
again otra vez
against contra
agenda el orden del día
agency la agencia
AIDS el Sida
air el aire
air conditioning el aire acondicionado
aircraft el avión
airline la compañía aérea
air mail por avión
air mattress la colchoneta
airport el aeropuerto
airport bus el autobús del aeropuerto
aisle el pasillo
alarm clock el despertador

alcohol el alcohol
Algeria Argelia
all todo; *all the streets* todas las calles; *that's all* eso es todo
allergic alérgico
alligator el caimán
almost casi
alone solo
already ya
always siempre
am: I am soy/estoy
Amazon: the Amazon Amazonas
ambulance la ambulancia
America Norteamérica
American americano
and y; (after 'i' or 'h') e
Andes los Andes, la sierra andina
ankle el tobillo
another otro
answering machine el contestador automático
antique shop el anticuario
antiseptic el antiséptico
apartment el departamento
aperitif el aperitivo
appetite el apetito
apple la manzana
application form la solicitud
appointment (business) la cita
apricot el albaricoque
April abril
are: you are (informal singular) eres/estás; (formal singular) es/está; (plural)

sois/estáis; *we are* somos/estamos; *they are* son/están
Argentina Argentina
Argentinian argentino
arm el brazo
arrive llegar
art el arte
art gallery la galería de arte
artichoke la alcachofa
artist el/la artista
as: as soon as possible lo antes posible
ashtray el cenicero
aspirin la aspirina
asthmatic asmático
at: at the post office en Correos; *at night* por la noche; *at 3 o'clock* a las tres
athletic shoes los trainers, los tenis
Atlantic Ocean el Océano Atlántico
ATM el cajero automático
attractive (person, offer) atractivo; (object) bonito
August agosto
aunt la tía
Australian australiano
automatic automático
available disponible
away: is it far away? ¿está lejos?; *go away!* ¡váyase!
awful horrible
ax el hacha

B

baby el bebé, el tierno (CAm); la guagua (Chi, Per)
baby carriage el cochecito
back (not front) la parte de atrás; (body) la espalda; to come back regresar
backpack la mochila
bacon el tocino; bacon and eggs huevos fritos con tocino
bad malo
bag la bolsa
bait el cebo
bake cocer al horno
balcony el balcón
ball la pelota
bakery la pastelería
banana el plátano
band (musicians) la banda
bandage la vendaje; (adhesive) la curita, la tirita
bank el banco
bank card la tarjeta de banco
banknote el billete (de banco)
bar (drinks) el bar; bar of chocolate la tableta de chocolate
barbecue la barbacoa
barber la peluquería de hombres
bargain la ganga
basement el sótano, la bodega
basin (sink) la fregadera
basket el canasta
basketball el baloncesto
bath la tina; to take a bath tomar un baño
bathroom el baño
battery (car) la batería, el acumulador (Mex); (flashlight, etc.) la pila
be (verb) ser
beach la playa
beach ball el balón de playa
beans los frijoles, los porotos (Chi, Arg, Uru)
beard la barba
beautiful hermoso
beauty products los productos de belleza
because porque
bed la cama
bed linen la ropa de cama
bedroom el dormitorio, la recámara
bedside lamp la lamparilla de noche

bedspread la colcha
beef la carne de vaca
beer la cerveza
before ... antes de ...
beginner el/la principiante
behind ... detrás de ...
beige beige
bell (church) la campana; (door) el timbre
below ... debajo de ...
belt el cinturón
beside al lado de
best (el) mejor
better mejor
between ... entre ...
bicycle la bicicleta
big grande
bill la cuenta
bird el pájaro
birthday el cumpleaños; happy birthday! ¡felicidades!
birthday present el regalo de cumpleaños
bite (by dog) la mordedura; (insect) la picadura; (verb: by dog) morder; (by insect) picar
bitter amargo
black negro
blackberries las moras
black currants las grosellas negras
blanket la manta, la cobija, la frazada (Mex, Ven, Chi, CAm)
bleach la lejía; (verb: hair) teñir
blind (cannot see) ciego
blinds las persianas
blister la ampolla
blond (adj) rubio, güero (Mex), catire (Cub, Ven, Col), chele (CAm)
blood la sangre
blood test el análisis de sangre
blouse la blusa
blue azul
boarding pass la tarjeta de embarque
boat el barco; (small) la barca
body el cuerpo
boil (of water) hervir; (egg, etc.) cocer
Bolivia Bolivia
Bolivian boliviano
boiled hervido
boiler el boiler
bolt (on door) el pasador; (verb) echar el pasador
bone el hueso
book el libro; (verb) reservar

bookstore la librería
boot (footwear) la bota
border el borde; (between countries) la frontera
boring aburrido
born: I was born in ... nací en ...
both: both of them los dos; both of us los dos; both ... and ... tanto ... como ...
bottle la botella
bottle opener el destapador
bottom el fondo; (part of body) el trasero
bowl (for animal) la cazuela; (for food) el tazón, la palangana (Arg, Uru)
box la caja
box office la taquilla
boy el chico, el joven, el chavo (Mex), el chaval (CAm), el pibe (Arg), el chamo (Ven)
boyfriend el novio
bra el sostén
bracelet la pulsera
brake el freno; (verb) frenar
brandy el coñac
Brazil Brasil
Brazilian brasileño
bread el pan
bread shop la panadería
breakdown (car) la descompostura
breakfast el desayuno
breathe respirar
bridge el puente; (game) el bridge
briefcase el portafolios
British británico
broken descompuesto, roto
brooch el broche
brother el hermano
brown café; (hair) castaño; (skin) moreno
bruise el cardenal
brush (hair) el cepillo del pelo; (paint) la brocha; (for cleaning) el cepillo; (verb: hair) cepillar el pelo
bucket el cubo
budget el presupuesto
building el edificio
bull el toro
bullfight la corrida de toros
bullfighter el torero
bullring la plaza de toros
bumper el parachoques, la defensa (Mex)
burglar el ladrón
burn la quemadura; (verb) quemar

bus el autobús; (local) el camión (Mex), la camioneta (Gua), el guagua (Cub), la micro, (Chi), la buseta (Col, Ecu)

business el negocio; *it's none of your business* no es asunto suyo

business card la tarjeta de vista

bus station la central de autobuses

busy (bar) concurrido; (phone) ocupado

but pero

butcher shop la carnicería

butter la mantequilla, la manteca (Arg, Uru)

button el botón

buy comprar

by: by the window junto a la ventana; *by Friday* para el viernes; *written by ...* escrito por ...

C

cabbage el repollo

cable car el teleférico

café la cafetería

cage la jaula

cake (small) el pastel, el queque (Chi, Per); (large) la tarta; *sponge cake* el bizcocho, el panqué (Col, Ven)

calculator la calculadora

call: what's it called? ¿cómo se llama?

camera la cámara fotográfica

camper trailer la camioneta

camper van la autocaravana

campfire la hoguera

campground el camping

camshaft el árbol de levas

can: can you ... ? ¿puede ...?; *I can't ...* no puedo ...

can (tin) la lata

Canada Canadá

Canadian canadiense

canal el canal

Canaries las (Islas) Canarias

candle la vela

candy los dulces

can opener el abrelatas

cap (bottle) el tapón; (hat) la gorra

car el auto, el automóvil, el carro

car (train) el vagón

carburetor el carburador

card la tarjeta

careful cuidadoso; *be careful!* ¡cuidado!

caretaker el portero, el encargado

carpenter el carpintero

carpet la alfombra

carrot la zanahoria

carry-on luggage el equipaje de mano

car seat (for baby/child) el portabebé

cart el carrito

case (suitcase) la maleta

cash el dinero; (verb) cobrar; *to pay cash* pagar al contado

cashier el cajero

cassette la cassette, la cinta

cassette player el cassette

castle el castillo

cat el gato

catch (bus, etc.) tomar

cathedral la catedral

Catholic (adj) católico

cauliflower la coliflor

cave la cueva

CD el disco compacto

ceiling el techo

cell phone el celular

cemetery el cementerio

center el centro

central heating la calefacción central

certificate el certificado

chair la silla

change (money) el suelto, el sencillo; (verb: money) cambiar; (clothes) cambiarse; (trains, etc.) hacer transbordo

charger el cargador

cheap barato

check el cheque

checkbook el libro de cheques

check-in (desk) la (mesa de) facturación

check in (verb) presentarse en la facturación

checkout la caja

cheers! (toast) ¡salud!

cheese el queso

cherry la cereza

chess el ajedrez

chest (body) el pecho; (furniture) el arcón

chest of drawers la cómoda

chewing gum el chicle

chicken el pollo, la gallina

child el niño/la niña

children los niños

children's ward la sala de pediatría

Chile Chile

Chilean chileno

chili el ají, el chile (Mex, CAm), el locoto (Bol, Per)

chimney la chimenea

china la porcelana

chips las patatas fritas

chocolate el chocolate; *box of chocolates* la caja de bombones

chop (food) la chuleta; (verb: cut) cortar

Christmas la navidad

church la iglesia

cigar el puro

cigarette el cigarrillo

city la ciudad

class la clase

classical music la música clásica

clean (adj) limpio

cleaner la muchacha

clear (obvious) evidente; (water) claro

clever listo

client el cliente

clock el reloj

close (near) cerca

close (verb) cerrar

closed cerrado

clothes la ropa

clubs (cards) los tréboles

coat el abrigo

coat hanger la percha

cocktail party el coctel

coffee el café

coin la moneda

cold (illness) el resfriado; (adj) frío; *I have a cold* estoy resfriado; *I'm cold* tengo frío

collar el cuello; (of animal) el collar

collection (stamps, etc.) la colección

Colombia Colombia

Colombian colombiano

color el color

color film la película en color

comb el peine; (verb) peinar

come venir; *I come from ...* soy de ...; *come here!* ¡acérquese!

comforter el edredón

compartment el compartimento

complicated complicado

computer la computadora

computer games los vídeo-juegos

concert el concierto

conditioner (hair) el acondicionador

condom el condón, el preservativo

condor el cóndor

conductor (bus) el cobrador; (orchestra) el director

conference la conferencia
conference room la sala de conferencias
congratulations! ¡enhorabuena!
consulate el consulado
contact lenses las lentes de contacto
contraceptive el anticonceptivo
contract el contrato
cook el cocinero/la cocinera; (verb) guisar
cookie la galleta
cool fresco
cork el corcho
corkscrew el sacacorchos
corner (of street) la esquina; (of room) el rincón
corner store la miscelánea
corridor el pasillo
cosmetics los cosméticos
cost (verb) costar; *what does it cost?* ¿cuánto cuesta?
Costa Rica Costa Rica
Costa Rican costarricense
cotton el algodón
cough la tos; (verb) toser
cough drops las pastillas para la garganta
countertop la encimera
country (state) el país; (not town) el campo
cousin el primo/la prima
crab el cangrejo
cramp el calambre
crazy loco
crayfish las cigalas
cream (dairy) la nata; (lotion) la crema
credit card la tarjeta de crédito
crib el capazo
crowded lleno (de gente)
cruise el crucero
crutches las muletas
cry (weep) llorar; (shout) gritar
Cuba Cuba
Cuban cubano
cucumber el pepino
cuff links los gemelos
cup la taza
cupboard el armario
curlers los rulos
curls los rizos
curtain la cortina
cushion el cojín
customs la aduana
cut la cortadura; (verb) cortar
cycling el ciclismo

D

dad papá
dairy products los productos lácteos
damp húmedo
dance el baile; (verb) bailar
dancer la bailadora
dangerous peligroso
dark oscuro; *dark blue* azul oscuro
daughter la hija
day el día
dead muerto
deaf sordo
dear (person) querido
December diciembre
deck chair la tumbona, la silla de extensión
decorator el pintor
deep profundo
delayed retrasado
deliberately a propósito
delicatessen la salchichonería
delivery la entrega
dentist el/la dentista
dentures la dentadura postiza
deny negar
deodorant el desodorante
department el departemento
department store la tienda de departamentos
departure la salida
departures las salidas
deposit el deposito
designer el diseñador/ la diseñadora
desk la mesa de escritorio
desert el desierto
dessert el postre
develop (film) revelar
diabetic diabético
diamonds (jewels; cards) los diamantes
diaper el pañal
diarrhea la diarrea
dictionary el diccionario
die morir
diesel (oil) el diesel, el gasoil (Ven), el petróleo (Arg)
different diferente; *that's different!* ¡eso es distinto!; *I'd like a different one* quisiera otro distinto
difficult difícil
dining room el comedor
dinner la cena
dinner party la cena
dirty sucio
disabled minusválido
discount descuento
dishwasher el lavavajillas
dishwashing liquid el lavavajillas
disposable diapers los pañales desechables
divorced divorciado
do hacer
doctor el médico/ la médica
document el documento
dog el perro
doll la muñeca
dollar el dólar
Dominican Dominicana
Dominican Republic República Dominicana
donkey el burro
door la puerta
double room la habitación doble
doughnut el dónut
down abajo
downward hacia abajo
downtown el centro (urbano)
dress el vestido
drink la bebida; (verb) beber, tomar; *would you like something to drink?* ¿quiere tomar algo?
drinking water el agua potable
drive (verb) manejar
driver el chofer
driver's license el carnet de conducir, el permiso de conducir, el brevete (Per, Col)
drunk borracho
dry seco
dry cleaner la tintorería
during durante
duster el trapo del polvo
duty-free libre de impuestos

E

each (every) cada; *300 pesos each* trescientos pesos cada uno
ear (inner) el oído; (outer) la oreja; *ears* las orejas
early temprano
earrings los aretes
east el oriente, el este
easy fácil
eat comer
Ecuador Ecuador
Ecuadorian ecuatoriano
egg el huevo, el blanquillo (CAm)
eggplant las berenjenas
eight ocho
eighteen dieciocho
eighty ochenta
either: either of them cualquiera de ellos; *either ... or ...* o bien ... o ...
elastic elástico
elbow el codo
electric eléctrico
electrician el/la electricista
electricity la electricidad

elevator el elevador

eleven once

El Salvador El Salvador

else: something else otra cosa; *someone else* otra persona; *somewhere else* en otra parte

email el email, el correo electrónico

email address la dirección de email

embarrassing avergonzante, penoso (Mex), violento (Arg)

embassy la embajada

emergency la emergencia

emergency brake (train) el freno de emergencia

emergency department el servicio de urgencias

emergency exit la salida de emergencia

employee el empleado

empty vacío

end el final

engaged (to be married) comprometido

engine (motor) el motor

engineering la ingeniería

England Inglaterra

English inglés

Englishman el inglés

Englishwoman la inglesa

enlargement la ampliación

enough bastante, suficiente

entertainment las diversiones

entrance la entrada

envelope el sobre

epileptic epiléptico

eraser la goma de borrar

escalator la escalera mecánica

especially sobre todo

estimate el presupuesto

evening la tarde

every cada; *every day* todos los días

everyone todos

everything todo

everywhere por todas partes

example el ejemplo; *for example* por ejemplo

excellent excelente

excess baggage exceso de equipaje

exchange (verb) cambiar

exchange rate el tipo de cambio

excursion la excursión

excuse me! (to get attention) ¡oiga, por favor!; (when sneezing, etc.) ¡disculpe!; *excuse me, please* (to get past) con permiso

executive el ejecutivo

exhaust el tubo de escape

exhibition la exposición

exit la salida

expensive caro

expressway la autopista

extension cord el cable alargador

eye el ojo

eyebrow la ceja

F

face la cara

faint (unclear) tenue; (verb) desmayarse; *I feel faint* estoy mareado

fair la feria; *it's not fair* no es justo

false teeth la dentadura postiza

fall (autumn) otoño (m)

family la familia

fan (handheld) el abanico; (ventilator) el ventilador; (soccer) el hincha; (enthusiast) el fanático

fantastic fantástico

far lejos; *how far is it to ... ?* ¿cuánto hay de aquí a ...?

fare el pasaje

farm (large) la hacienda, la estancia (Arg, Uru); (small) la finca, el rancho (Mex), la chacra (Arg)

fashion la moda

fast rápido

fat (adj) gordo; (on meat, etc.) la grasa

father el padre

faucet la llave

fax el fax; (verb: document) enviar por fax

February febrero

feel (touch) tocar; *I feel hot* tengo calor; *I feel like ...* me apetece ...; *I don't feel well* no me encuentro bien

fence la cerca

ferry el ferry

festival la fiesta

fiancé el prometido

fiancée la prometida

field (grass) el campo; (of study) la especialidad

fifteen quince

fifty cincuenta

fig el higo

figures los números

filling (tooth) el empaste; (sandwich, cake) el relleno

film la película

filter el filtro

filter papers los papeles de filtro

finger el dedo

fire el fuego; (blaze) el incendio

fire extinguisher el extintor

fireplace la chimenea

fireworks los fuegos artificiales

first primero

first aid primeros auxilios

first class de primera

first floor el primer piso

first name el nombre de pila

fish el pez; (food) el pescado

fishing la pesca; *to go fishing* ir a pescar

fishmonger la pescadería

five cinco

flag la bandera

flash (camera) el flash

flashlight la linterna

flat (level) plano; (apartment) el departamento; *flat tire* la rueda pinchada

flavor el sabor

flea la pulga

flea spray el spray antipulgas

flight el vuelo

floor (el suelo); (story) el piso

florist la florería

flour la harina

flower la flor

flowerbed el arriate

flute la flauta; (wooden,, etc.) la quena

fly (insect) la mosca; (verb: of plane, insect) volar; (of person) viajar en avión

fog la niebla

folk music la música folklórica

food la comida

food poisoning la intoxicación alimenticia

foot el pie

for: for me para mí; *what for?* ¿para qué?; *for a week* (para) una semana

foreigner el extranjero/ la extranjera

forest el bosque; (tropical) la selva

forget olvidar

fork el tenedor; (garden) la horquilla

forty cuarenta

fountain la fuente

fountain pen la (pluma) estilográfica

four cuatro

fourteen catorce

fourth cuarto

free (unoccupied) libre; (no charge) gratis

freezer el congelador

French francés

french fries las papas fritas

Friday viernes

fried frito

friend el amigo/la amiga

friendly amable

front: in front of ... delante de ...

frost la escarcha

frozen foods los congelados

fruit la fruta

fruit juice el jugo de frutas

fry freír

frying pan la sartén

full lleno; I'm full estoy lleno

full board pensión completa

funny divertido; (odd) raro

furniture los muebles

G

garage (for repairs) el taller, el garaje; (for gas) la gasolinera, el grifo (Per); (for parking) el garage, la cochera (Mex)

garbage la basura

garbage bag la bolsa de basura

garbage can el cubo de la basura, el balde de la basura

garden el jardín

garden center el vivero

garlic el ajo

gasoline la gasolina, la nafta (Arg), la bencina (Chi)

gas-permeable lenses las lentes de contacto semi-rígidas

gas station la gasolinera

gate la puerta; (at airport) la puerta de embarque

gay (homosexual) gay

gearbox la caja de cambios

gear stick la palanca de velocidades

gel (hair) el gel

German alemán

get (fetch) traer; do you have ... ? ¿tiene ...?; to get the train tomar el tren

get back: we get back tomorrow mañana estaremos de regreso; to get something back recobrar algo

get in (of train, etc.) subirse; (of person) llegar

get off (bus, etc.) bajarse

get on (bus, etc.) subirse

get out bajarse; (bring out) sacar

get up (rise) levantarse

gift el regalo

gin la ginebra

ginger (spice) el jengibre

girl la chica, la joven, la chavala (CAm), la chava (Mex), la piba (Arg), la chama (Ven)

girlfriend la novia

give dar

glad contento

glass (material) el vidrio; (for drinking) el vaso, la copa

glasses los lentes, los anteojos, las gafas

gloves los guantes

glue el pegamento

go ir

gold el oro

good bueno; good! ¡bien!

good afternoon buenas tardes

goodbye adiós, hasta luego

good evening buenas noches

good morning buenos días

government el gobierno

granddaughter la nieta

grandfather el abuelo

grandmother la abuela

grandparents los abuelos

grandson el nieto

grapes las uvas

grass la hierba

gray gris

Great Britain Gran Bretaña

green verde

greengrocer la verdulería

grill la parrilla

grilled a la plancha

grocery store los abarrotes, el almacén, el boliche (Chi, Arg, Uru), la pulpería (Cos, ElS), la bodega (Gua, Nic)

ground floor la planta baja, el primer piso

groundsheet la lona impermeable, el suelo aislante

guarantee la garantía; (verb) garantizar

Guatemalan guatemalteco

guest la invitada

guide el/la guía

guidebook la guía turística

guided tour la visita con guía

guitar la guitarra

gun (rifle) el fusil; (pistol) la pistola

gym el centro deportivo

H

hair el pelo, el cabello

haircut el corte de pelo

hair salon la peluquería

hairdryer el secador (de pelo)

hairspray la laca

half medio; half an hour media hora

half-board media pensión

ham el jamón

hamburger la hamburguesa

hammer el martillo

hand la mano

handbag el bolso, la cartera

handbrake el freno de mano

handle (door) la manilla

handshake el apretón de manos

handsome lindo, guapo

handyman el albañil

hangover la resaca

happy contento

harbor el puerto

hard duro; (difficult) difícil

hardware store la ferretería

hat el sombrero; (woolen) el gorro

have tener; I don't have ... no tengo ...; do you have ... ? ¿tiene ...?; I have to go tengo que irme ; can I have ... ? ¿me da ...?

hay fever la fiebre del heno

he él

head la cabeza

headache el dolor de cabeza

headlights los faros

headphones los auriculares

hear escuchar

hearing aid el audífono

heart el corazón

hearts (cards) los corazones

heater la estufa

heating la calefacción
heavy pesado
heel el talón; (shoe) el tacón
hello hola; (on phone) dígame, bueno (Mex), hola (Arg), aló (Ven)
help la ayuda; (verb) ayudar
hepatitis la hepatitis
her: it's for her es para ella; *give it to her* déselo; *her book* su libro; *her shoes* sus zapatos; *it's hers* es suyo
high alto
highway la autopista
hiking el senderismo
hill el cerro
him: it's for him es para él; *give it to him* déselo
his: his book su libro; *his shoes* sus zapatos; *it's his* es suyo
history la historia
HIV-positive seropositivo
hobby el pasatiempos
home: at home en casa
homeopathy la homeopatía
Honduran hondureño
Honduras Honduras
honest honrado; (sincere) sincero
honey la miel
honeymoon la luna de miel
hood (car) el cofre (Mex), el capó, el capote
horn (car) el claxon; (animal) el cuerno
horrible horrible
horse el caballo
hospital el hospital
hostess la anfitriona
hot caliente; (weather) caluroso; (spicy) picante
hour la hora
house la casa
household products los productos del hogar
how? ¿cómo?
how are you? ¿qué tal?
humid húmedo
hundred cien
hungry: I'm hungry tengo hambre
hurry: I'm in a hurry tengo prisa
husband el marido

I

I yo
ice el hielo
ice cream el helado, el sorbete (CAm)
ice pop la paleta

if si
ignition el encendido
immediately en seguida, al tiro (Chi)
impossible imposible
in en; *in English* en inglés; *in the hotel* en el hotel; *in Lima* en Lima; *he's not in* no está
included incluido
indigestion indigestión
inexpensive barato
infection la infección
information la información
inhaler (for asthma, etc.) el inhalador
injection la inyección
injury la herida
ink la tinta
inn la fonda
inner tube la llanta
insect el insecto
insect repellent la loción anti-mosquitos
insomnia el insomnio
instant coffee el café instantáneo
insurance el seguro
interesting interesante
Internet el internet
interpret interpretar
interpreter el/la intérprete
invitation la invitación
invoice la factura
Ireland Irlanda
Irish irlandés/irlandesa
iron (material) el hierro; (for clothes) la plancha; (verb) planchar
is es/está
island la isla
it lo/la, el/ella
its su

J

jacket el saco
jam la mermelada
January enero
jazz el jazz
jeans los vaqueros
jellyfish la medusa
jeweler (shop) la joyería
job el trabajo
jog (verb) hacer footing
jogging suit el sudadera, el mono (Ven), los pants (Mex)
joke la broma
journey el viaje
juice el jugo
July julio
June junio
jungle la selva

just (only) sólo; *it's just arrived* acaba de llegar

K

kerosene el querosén, el queroséno
key la llave
keyboard el teclado
kidney el riñón
kilo el kilo
kilometer el kilómetro
kitchen la cocina
knee la rodilla
knife el cuchillo
knitwear los artículos de punto
know saber; (person, place) conocer; *I don't know* no sé

L

label la etiqueta
lace el encaje
laces (shoe) los cordones (de los zapatos)
lady la señora
lake el lago
lamb el cordero
lamp la lámpara
lampshade la pantalla
land la tierra; (verb) aterrizar
language el idioma
large grande
last (final) último; *last week* la semana pasada; *at last!* ¡por fin!
late: it's getting late se está haciendo tarde; *the bus is late* el autobús está atrasado
later más tarde
Latin America América Latina
laugh reír
laundromat la lavandería automática
laundry (dirty) la ropa sucia; (washed) la colada
laundry detergent el detergente
law el derecho
lawn el pasto
lawn mower la maquina podadora
lawyer el abogado/ la abogada
laxative el laxante
lazy flojo
leaf la hoja
leaflet el folleto
learn aprender
leash (for dog) la correa
leather el cuero

lecture hall
el anfiteatro

left (not right)
izquierdo; *there's nothing left* no queda nada

leg la pierna

lemon el limón

lemonade la limonada

length el largo

lens la lente

less menos

lesson la clase

letter (mail) la carta; (of alphabet) la letra

lettuce la lechuga

library la biblioteca

license el permiso

license plate la matrícula, la placa, la chapa (Arg)

life la vida

light la luz; (adj: not heavy) ligero; (not dark) claro

light bulb la bombilla, el foco (Mex), la lamparita (Arg), el bombillo (Col)

lighter el encendedor

lighter fuel el gas para el encendedor

light meter el fotómetro

like: I like ... me gusta ...; *I like swimming* me gusta nadar; *it's like ...* es como ...; *like this one* como éste

lime (fruit) la lima, el limón

line (phone, etc.) línea; la cola; (verb) hacer cola

lipstick el lapiz labial

liqueur el licor

list la lista

literature la literatura

liter el litro

litter la basura

little (small) pequeño; *it's a little big* es un poco grande; *just a little* sólo un poquito

liver el hígado

living room la sala

lizard la lagartija; (large) el lagarto

lobster la langosta

lollipop el chupete

long largo

lost property office la oficina de objetos perdidos

lot: a lot mucho

loud alto

lounge (in house) la sala; (in hotel, etc.) el salón

love el amor; (verb) querer; *I love Mexico* me encanta México

low bajo

luck la suerte; *good luck!* ¡suerte!

luggage el equipaje

luggage rack la rejilla de equipajes

lunch la comida, el almuerzo

M

madam señora

magazine la revista

maid la recamarera

mail el correo; *to mail* echar al correo

mailbox el buzón

mail carrier el cartero

main course el plato principal

main road la calle principal

make hacer

makeup el maquillaje

man el hombre

manager el/la gerente

many: not many no muchos

map el mapa

marble el mármol

March marzo

margarine la margarina

market el mercado, la feria (Arg, Uru), el tianguis (Mex)

married casado

mascara el rímel

match (light) la cerilla, el fósforo; (sports) el partido

material (cloth) la tela

matter: it doesn't matter no importa

mattress el colchón

May mayo

maybe quizás

me: it's for me es para mí; *give it to me* démelo

meal la comida

mean: what does this mean? ¿qué significa esto?

meat la carne

mechanic el mecánico

medicine la medicina

medium-dry (wine) semi-seco

meeting la reunión

melon el melón

menu la carta

message el recado

metro station le estación de metro

Mexican mexicano

Mexico México

Mexico City la Ciudad de México, el Distrito Federal (Mex)

microwave el microondas

middle: in the middle en el centro

midnight la medianoche

milk la leche

mine: it's mine es mío

mineral water el agua mineral

minute el minuto

mirror el espejo

Miss Señorita

mistake la equivocación

modem el modem

Monday lunes

money el dinero

monkey el mono, el mico

monitor el monitor

month el mes

monument el monumento

moon la luna

moped el ciclomotor

more más

morning la mañana; *in the morning* por la mañana

mosaic el mosaico

mosquito el mosquito, el zancudo (Mex)

motel el motel

mother la madre

motorboat la motora

motorcycle la motocicleta

mountain la montaña, la sierra

mountain bike la bicicleta de montaña

mountain range la sierra, la cordillera (Chi)

mouse el ratón

mousse (for hair) la mousse

mouth la boca

move (verb: something) mover; (oneself) moverse; *don't move!* ¡no se mueva!

movie la película

movie theater el cine

Mr. Señor

Mrs. Señora

much: much better mucho mejor; *much slower* mucho más despacio

mud el lodo

mum mamá

museum el museo

mushrooms los hongos

music la música

musical instrument el instrumento musical

musician el músico

music system el equipo de música

mussels los mejillones, las cholgas (Chi)

must: I must ... tengo que ...

mustache el bigote

mustard la mostaza

muzzle el bozal

my: my book mi libro; *my keys* mis llaves

N

nail (metal) el clavo; (finger) la uña
nail clippers el cortauñas
nailfile la lima de uñas
nail polish el esmalte de uñas
name el nombre; what's your name? ¿cómo se llama usted?; my name is... me llamo...
napkin la servilleta
narrow estrecho
Native American el/la indígena; (adj) indígena
near: near the door junto a la puerta; near New York cerca de New York
necessary necesario
neck el cuello
necklace el collar
need (verb) necesitar; I need ... necesito ...; there's no need no hace falta
needle la aguja
negative (photo) el negativo
nephew el sobrino
never nunca
new nuevo
news las noticias
newspaper el periódico, el diario
newsstand el kiosko de periódicos
New Zealand Nueva Zelanda
New Zealander el neozelandés/ la neozelandesa; (adj) neozelandés
next siguiente; next week la semana que viene; what next? ¿y ahora qué?
Nicaragua Nicaragua
Nicaraguan nicaragüense
nice (place) agradable; (person) simpático; (to eat) bueno, rico, sabroso
niece la sobrina
night la noche
nightclub la caberé, la peña
nightgown el camisón
nightstand la mesilla de noche
nine nueve
nineteen diecinueve
ninety noventa
no (response) no; I have no money no tengo dinero
nobody nadie
noisy ruidoso
noon el mediodía

north el norte
North America América del norte, Norteamérica
North American norteamericano
Northern Ireland Irlanda del Norte
nose la nariz
not no; he's not ... no es/está ...
notebook el cuaderno
notepad el bloc
nothing nada
novel la novela
November noviembre
now ahora
nowhere en ninguna parte
number el número
nurse el enfermo/ la enferma
nut (fruit) la nuez; (for bolt) la tuerca

O

occasionally de vez en cuando
occupied ocupado
October octubre
octopus el pulpo
of de
office (place) la oficina; (room) el despacho
office block el bloque de oficinas
often con frecuencia
oil el aceite
ointment la pomada
OK okey, de acuerdo
old viejo; how old are you? ¿cuántos años tiene?
olive la aceituna, la oliva
olive oil el aceite de oliva
olive tree el olivo
omelet la tortilla de huevos
on ... en ...
one uno/una
onion la cebolla
only sólo
open (adj) abierto; (verb) abrir
opening times el horario de apertura
operating room el quirófano
operation la operación, la intervención quirúrgica
operator la operadora
optician el/la oculista
or o
orange (fruit) la naranja; (color) naranja
orange juice el jugo de naranja
orchestra la orquesta

order el pedido
ordinary corriente
other: the other (one) el otro
our nuestro; it's ours es nuestro
out: he's out no está
outside fuera
oven el horno, la estufa
over ... encima de ...; (more than) más de ...; it's over the road está al otro lado de la calle; when the party is over cuando termine la fiesta; over there por allá
overpass el paso elevado
oyster la ostra

P

Pacific Ocean el Océano Pacífico
package el paquete
packet el paquete; (cigarettes) la cajetilla; (candy, chips) la bolsa
padlock el candado
page la página
pain el dolor
paint la pintura
pair el par
pajamas el piyama
palace el palacio
pale pálido
palm tree la palmera
Panama Panamá
Panama Canal el canal de Panamá
Panamanian panameño
pancakes los panqueques
panpipes la zampoña
pants los pantalones
pantyhose las pantimedias
paper el papel; (newspaper) el periódico
Paraguay Paraguay
Paraguayan paraguayo
pardon? ¿cómo dice?
parents los padres
park el parque; (verb) estacionar; no parking prohibido estacionar
parking lot el estacionamiento
parsley el perejil
part (hair) la raya
party (celebration) la fiesta; (group) el grupo; (political) el partido
pass (in car) rebasar, adelantar
passenger el pasajero

passport el pasaporte
password la contraseña
pasta la pasta
path el camino
pavement la banqueta
pay pagar
payment el pago
peach el melocotón
peanuts los cacahuetes, los cacahuates, el maní
pear la pera
pearl la perla
peas los chícharos, las arvejas (Arg, Bol, Chi, Col), los guirantes (Ven)
pedestrian el peatón; *pedestrian zone* la zona peatonal
peg la pinza, el gancho
pen la pluma
pencil el lápiz
pencil sharpener el sacapuntas
penknife la navaja
pen pal el amigo/ la amiga por correspondencia
people la gente
pepper la pimienta; (red, green) el pimiento
per: per night por noche
perfect perfecto
perfume el perfume
perhaps quizás
perm la permanente
Peru Perú
Peruvian peruano
peso el peso
pets los animales de compañía, los animales domésticos
pharmacy la farmacia*phone book* la guía telefónica
phone booth la cabina telefónica
phone card la tarjeta telefónica
photocopier la fotocopiadora
photograph la foto(grafía); (verb) fotografiar
photographer el fotógrafo
phrasebook el libro de frases
piano el piano
pickpocket el carterista
pickup (postal) la recogida
picnic el picnic
piece el pedazo
pig el cerdo, el chancho, el tunco (CAm)
pill la pastilla
pillow la almohada
pilot el piloto
PIN el número personal
pin el alfiler

pineapple la piña, el ananás (Arg)
pink rosa
pipe (for smoking) la pipa; (for water) la tubería
piston el piston
place el lugar; *at your place* en su casa
plant la planta
plastic el plástico
plastic bag la bolsa de plástico
plate el plato
platform (train) el andén
play (theater) la pieza; (verb) jugar
please por favor
pleased to meet you encantado/encantada
plug (sink) el tapón; (electrical) el enchufe
plumber el plomero
pocket el bolsillo
poison el veneno
police la policía
police officer el policía
police report la denuncia
police station la comisaría
politics la política
poor pobre; (bad quality) malo
pop music la música pop
pork la carne de cerdo/chancho
port (harbor) el puerto; (drink) el oporto
porter (hotel) el portero
Portuguese portugués
possible posible
postcard la postal
poster el póster
post office (la oficina de) Correos
potato la papa
poultry las aves
pound (money) la libra; (weight) la libra
powder el polvo; (make up) los polvos
prefer preferir
pregnant embarazada
prescription la receta
pretty bonito; (quite) bastante
price el precio
priest el cura
printer la impresora
private privado
problem el problema
profession la profesión
professor el profesor
profits los beneficios
prohibited prohibido
protection factor (SPF) el factor de protección
public público; *public holiday* el día de fiesta; *public*

swimming pool la piscina municipal
Puerto Rican puertorriqueño
Puerto Rico Puerto Rico
pull tirar de
puncture el pinchazo, la ponchadura (Mex)
purple morado
purse la cartera, el monedero
push empujar
put poner
pyramid la pirámide

Q

quality la calidad
quarter el cuarto
question la pregunta
quick rápido
quiet tranquilo; (person) callado
quite (fairly) bastante; (fully) completamente

R

rabbit el conejo
radiator el radiador
radio la radio
radish el rábano
rake el rastrillo
railroad el ferrocarril
rain la lluvia
raincoat el impermeable
rainforest la selva tropical
raisins las pasas
raspberry la frambuesa
rare (uncommon) insólito; (steak) poco cocido
rash el salpullido
rat la rata
razor blades las hojas de afeitar
read leer
ready listo
receipt el recibo
reception la recepción
receptionist el/la recepcionista
record (music) el disco; (sports, etc.) el récord
record player el tocadiscos
record store la tienda de discos
red rojo; (wine) tinto
refreshments el refrigerio
refrigerator el refrigerador, la nevera
registered mail correo certificado
relative el pariente
relax relajarse; (rest) descansar
religion la religión

remember: I remember recuerdo; *I don't remember* no recuerdo

rent alquilar, arrendar

repair arreglar

report el informe

reservation la reservación

rest (remainder) el resto; (verb: relax) descansar

restrooms baños; (men) los baños de caballeros; (women) los baños de señoras

restaurant el restaurante

restaurant car el vagón-restaurante

return (come back) volver; (give back) devolver

rice el arroz

rich rico

right (correct) correcto; (not left) derecho

ring (jewelry.) el anillo

ripe maduro

river el río

road la carretera, la calle

roasted asado

robbery el robo

rock (stone) la roca; (music) el rock

roll (bread) el bolillo

roof el tejado, el techo

room la habitación, el cuarto; (space) el espacio

room service el servicio de habitaciones

rope la cuerda

rose la rosa

round (circular) redondo

roundabout la glorieta

round-trip ticket el boleto/ pasaje de ida y vuelta

row (verb) remar

rubber (material) la hule

ruby (gem) el rubí

rug (mat) la alfombra, el tapete; (blanket) la cobija, la manta, la frazada (Mex, Ven, Chi, CAm)

rugby el rugby

ruins las ruinas

ruler (for measuring) la regla

rum el ron

run (verb) correr

runway la pista

S

sad triste

safe (not dangerous) seguro

safety pin el alfiler de gancho

sailboard la tabla de windsurfing

sailboat el balandro

sailing la vela

salad la ensalada

sale (at reduced prices) las rebajas

sales las ventas

salmon el salmón

salt la sal

Salvadorean salvadoreño

same: the same dress el mismo vestido; *the same people* la misma gente; *same again, please* otro igual, por favor

sand la arena

sandals las sandalias, los guaraches (Mex), las ojotas (Bol, Per, Ecu)

sand dunes las dunas

sandwich el sandwich

sanitary napkins las compresas

Saturday sábado

sauce la salsa

saucepan la olla

saucer el platillo

sauna la sauna

sausage la salchicha

say decir; *what did you say?* ¿qué ha dicho?; *how do you say ... ?* ¿cómo se dice ...?

scarf la bufanda; (head) el pañuelo

schedule el program, (bus, etc.) el horario

school la escuela

science las ciencias

scissors las tijeras

Scotland Escocia

Scottish escocés/escocesa

screen la pantalla

screw el tornillo

screwdriver el destornillador

sea el mar

seafood los mariscos

seat el asiento

seat belt el cinturón de seguridad

second el segundo; *second class* de segunda

see ver; *I can't see* no veo; *I see* entiendo

self-employed el autónomo/la autónoma

sell vender

seminar el seminario

send mandar

separate (adj) distinto

separated separado

September septiembre

serious serio

seven siete

seventeen diecisiete

seventy setenta

several varios

sew coser

shampoo el champú

shave el afeitado; *to shave* afeitarse, rasurarse

shaving foam la espuma de afeitar

shawl el rebozo

she ella

sheet la sábana; (of paper) la hoja

shell la concha

shellfish los mariscos

sherry el jerez

ship el barco

shirt la camisa

shoelaces los cordones de los zapatos, las agujetas (Mex)

shoe polish la crema de zapatos

shoes los zapatos

shoe store la zapatería

shopping la compra; *to go shopping* ir de compras

short corto; (height) bajo

shorts los pantalones cortos, los shorts

shoulder el hombro

shower (bath) la regardera; (rain) el chubasco (Mex)

shower gel el gel de ducha, el gel de baño

shrimp los camarones, las gambas

shutter (camera) el obturador; (window) el postigo

sick: I feel sick siento náuseas; *to be sick* (vomit) devolver

side (edge) el borde

side lights los pilotos

sightseeing el turismo

silk la seda

silver (metal) la plata; (color) plateado

simple sencillo

sing cantar

single (ticket) de ida; (only) único; (unmarried) soltero

single room el cuarto individual

sink el fregadero

sister la hermana

six seis

sixteen dieciséis

sixty sesenta

skid patinar

skiing: to go skiing ir a esquiar

skin cleanser la leche limpiadora

ski resort la estación de esquí

skirt la falda, la pollera (Arg, Bol)

skis los esquís

sky el cielo

sleep el sueño; (verb) dormir

sleeper car el coche-cama

sleeping bag el saco de dormir

sleeping pill el somnífero

sleeve la manga

slip (underwear) la combinación

slippers las zapatillas

slow lento

small chico

smell el olor; (verb) oler

smile la sonrisa; (verb) sonreír

smoke el humo; (verb) fumar

snack la merienda

snow la nieve

so: so good tan bueno; *not so much* no tanto

soaking solution (for contact lenses) la solución limpiadora

soap el jabón

soccer el futbol; (ball) el balón

socks los calcetines

soda water la soda

sofa el sofa

soft blando

soil la tierra

somebody alguien

somehow de alguna manera

something algo

sometimes a veces

somewhere en alguna parte

son el hijo

song la canción

sorry! ¡disculpe!; *I'm sorry* perdón/lo siento; *sorry?* (pardon) ¿cómo dice?

soup la sopa

south el sur

South America América del Sur

souvenir el recuerdo

spade la pala

spades (cards) las picas

Spain España

Spaniard el español/la española; *the Spanish* los españoles

sparkling water el agua con gas

speak hablar; *do you speak ... ?* ¿habla ...?; *I don't speak ...* no hablo ...; *I'd like to speak to...* quisiera hablar con...

speed la velocidad

speed limit el límite de velocidad

spider la araña

spinach las espinacas

spoon la cuchara

sports el deporte

spring (mechanical) el resorte; (season) la primavera

square (in town) la plaza; (adj) cuadrado

staircase la escalera

stairs las escaleras

stamp la estampilla, el timbre (Mex)

stapler la engrapadora

star la estrella

start el principio; (verb) empezar

starters el primer plato

statement la declaración

station la estación

statue la estatua

steak el filete

steal robar; *it's been stolen* lo llevaron

steamed al vapor

steamer (boat) el vapor

stepdaughter la hijastra

stepfather el padastro

stepmother la madastra

stepson el hijastro

still water el agua sin gas

stockings las medias

stomach el estómago

stomachache el dolor de estómago

stop (bus) la parada; (verb) parar; *stop!* ¡alto!

store la tienda, el almacén

storm la tormenta

stove la estufa, la cocina, el horno

stove fuel el camping-gas

strawberries las fresas

stream (small river) el arroyo

street la calle

string la cuerda

stroller la sillita de ruedas

strong fuerte

student el/la estudiante

stuffy sofocante

stupid bruto

suburbs las afueras

subway el metro, el subte (Arg)

sugar el azúcar

suit (clothing) el traje, el terno (Chi); *it suits you* te sienta bien

suitcase la maleta

summer el verano

sun el sol

sunbathe tomar el sol

sunburn la quemadura de sol

Sunday domingo

sunglasses los lentes de sol

sunny: it's sunny hace sol

sunshade la sombrilla

sunstroke la insolación

suntan: to get a suntan broncearse

suntan lotion la loción bronceadora

suntanned bronceado

supermarket el supermercado

supper la cena

supplement el suplemento

suppository el supositorio

sure seguro

surname el apellido

suspenders (clothes) los tirantes

sweat el sudor; (verb) sudar

sweater el suéter el jersey, la chompa (Per, Bol), el buzo (Arg, Uru)

sweatshirt la sudadera

sweet (not sour) dulce; (sherry) oloroso

swim (verb) nadar

swimming la natación

swimming pool la piscina, la alberca, la pileta

swimming trunks el bañador

swimsuit el bañador, el traje de baño

switch el interruptor

synagogue la sinagoga

syringe la jeringa

syrup el jarabe

T

table la mesa

tablet la pastilla

take tomar

take off el despegue

talcum powder los polvos de talco

talk la charla; (verb) conversar, hablar, platicar (Mex)

tall alto

tampons los tampones

tangerine la mandarina

tapestry el tapiz

taxi el taxi

taxi stand el sitio de taxis

tea el té

teacher el profesor/la profesora

teakettle el hervidor de agua

technician el técnico

telephone el teléfono; (verb) llamar por teléfono

television la televisión
temperature la temperatura; (fever) la fiebre
ten diez
tennis el tenis
tent la carpa, la tienda
tent peg la estaquilla, la estaca
tent pole el mástil
terminal la terminal
terrace la terraza
test la prueba
than que
thank (verb) agradecer; *thank you* gracias; *thanks* gracias
that: that one ése/ésa; *that bus* ese autobús; *that man* ese hombre; *that woman* esa mujer; *what's that?* ¿qué es eso?; *I think that ...* creo que ...
the el/la; (plural) los/las
theater el teatro
their: their room su habitación; *their books* sus libros; *it's theirs* es suyo
them: it's for them es para ellos/ellas; *give it to them* déselo
then (at that time) en aquel entonces; (after) después, luego
there allí; *there is/are ...* hay ...; *is/are there ... ?* ¿hay ...?
these: these men estos hombres; *these women* estas mujeres; *these are mine* éstos son míos
they ellos/ellas
thick grueso
thief el ladrón
thin delgado
think pensar; *I think so* creo que sí; *I'll think about it* lo pensaré
third tercero
thirsty: I'm thirsty tengo sed
thirteen trece
thirty treinta
this: this one éste/ésta; *this man* este hombre; *this woman* esta mujer; *what's this?* ¿qué es esto?; *this is Mr. ...* éste es el señor ...
those: those men esos hombres; *those women* esas mujeres
thousand mil
throat la garganta

through por
three tres
thunderstorm la tormenta
Thursday jueves
ticket (train, etc.) el boleto, el pasaje; (theater, etc.) la entrada
ticket office la taquilla
tide la marea
tie la corbata; (verb) atar
tight ajustado
time tiempo; *what time is it?* ¿qué hora es?
tin el bote, la lata
tip (money) la propina; (end) la punta
tire la llanta
tired cansado
tire iron la llave de las tuercas
tissues los klínex
to: to America a América; *to the station* a la estación; *to the doctor* al médico
toast el pan tostado
tobacco el tabaco
today hoy
together juntos
toilet la taza
toilet paper el papel higiénico
tomato el jitomate
tomato juice el jugo de jitomate
tomorrow mañana
tongue la lengua
tonic la tónica
tonight esta noche
too (also) también; (excessively) demasiado
tooth el diente; *back tooth* la muela
toothache el dolor de muelas
toothbrush el cepillo de dientes
toothpaste la pasta de dientes
tour la excursión
tourist el/la turista
tourist office la oficina de turismo
towel la toalla
tower la torre
town el pueblo, la ciudad
town hall el ayuntamiento
toy el juguete
trade fair la feria
tractor el tractor
tradition la tradición
traffic la circulación
traffic jam el embotellamiento

traffic lights el semáforo
trailer la caravana, el remolque
train el tren
trainee el aprendiz
translate traducir
translator el traductor/ la traductora
trash can el contendor de basura
travel agency la agencia de viajes
traveler's check el cheque de viajero
tray la bandeja
tree el árbol
truck el camión
true cierto; *it's true* es cierto
trunk (car) la cajuela (Mex), la maleta, el maletero, el baúl (Per)
try intentar
Tuesday martes
tunnel el túnel
turn (left/right) dé vuelta (a la izquierda/derecha)
turn: it's my turn me toca a mí
turn signal la direccional
tweezers las pinzas
twelve doce
twenty veinte
two dos
typewriter la máquina de escribir

U

ugly feo
umbrella el paraguas
uncle el tío
under ... debajo de ...
underpants los calconcillos
understand entender; *I don't understand* no entiendo
underwear la ropa interior
United States Estados Unidos
university la universidad
unleaded sin plomo
until hasta
unusual raro, extraño
up arriba; (upward) hacia arriba
urgent urgente
us: it's for us es para nosotros/nosotras; *give it to us* dénoslo
use el uso; (verb) usar; *it's no use* no sirve de nada

useful útil
usual corriente
usually en general, normalmente

V

vacancies (rooms) cuartos libres
vacation las vacaciones
vaccination la vacuna
vacuum cleaner la aspiradora
valley el valle
valve la válvula
vanilla la vainilla
vase la válvula
veal la (carne de) ternera
vegetables las verduras
vegetarian vegetariano
vehicle el vehículo
Venezuela Venezuela
Venezuelan venezolano
very muy; *very much* mucho
vest la camiseta
vet el veterinario
video (tape) la cinta de vídeo; (film) el vídeo
video games los vídeo-juegos
video recorder el (aparato de) vídeo
view la vista
viewfinder el visor de imagen
villa el chalet
village el pueblo
vinegar el vinagre
violin el violín
visit la visita; (verb) visitar
visiting hours las horas de visita
visitor el/la visita
vitamin pills las vitaminas
vodka el vodka
voice la voz
voicemail la mensajería de voz
volcano el volcán
vulture el zopilote

W

wait (verb) esperar; *wait!* ¡espere!
waiter el mozo, el mesero (Mex, CAm), la garzona (Arg, Uru, Chi); *waiter!* ¡señor!
waiting room la sala de espera
waitress la moza, la mesera (Mex, CAm) la garzona (Arg, Uru, Chi); *waitress!* ¡señorita!
Wales Gales

walk (stroll) el paseo; (verb) caminar; *to go for a walk* ir de paseo
wall la pared; (outside) el muro
wallet la cartera, la billetera
want (verb) querer
war la guerra
wardrobe el armario
warm caliente; (weather) caluroso
was estaba/era
washing machine la zapatilla
wasp la avispa
watch el reloj; (verb) mirar
water el agua
waterfall la cascada
water heater el calentador (de agua)
wave la ola; (verb) agitar
wavy (hair) ondulado
we nosotros/nosotras
weather el tiempo
website la web site, el sitio web
wedding la boda
Wednesday miércoles
weeds las malas hierbas
week la semana
welcome bienvenido; (verb) dar la bienvenida; *you're welcome* no hay de qué
wellington boots las botas de hule
Welsh galés/galesa
were: you were (informal singular) eras/estabas; (formal singular) era/estaba; (informal plural) erais/estáis; (formal plural) eran/estaban; *we were* éramos/estábamos; *they were* eran/estaban
west el occidente
wet mojado
what? ¿qué?
wheel la rueda
wheelchair la silla de ruedas
when? ¿cuándo?
where? ¿dónde?
whether si
which? ¿cuál?
whiskey el whisky
white blanco
who? ¿quién?
why? ¿por qué?
wide ancho; *3 meters wide* de tres metros de ancho
wife la esposa
wind el viento
window la ventana

windshield el parabrisas
wine el vino
wine list la carta de vinos
wine merchant el vinatero
wing el ala
winter el invierno
with con
without sin
witness el testigo
woman la mujer
wood (material) la madera
wool la lana
word la palabra
work el trabajo; (verb) trabajar; (function) funcionar
worse peor
worst (el) peor
wrapping paper el papel de envolver; (for presents) el papel de regalo
wrench la llave inglesa
wrist la muñeca
writing paper el papel de escribir
wrong equivocado

X, Y, Z

X-ray department el servicio de radiología
xylophone (wooden) la marimba
year el año
yellow amarillo
yes sí
yesterday ayer
yet todavía; *not yet* todavía no
yogurt el yogur
you usted; (informal) tú, vos (Arg, Uru, Par); (plural) ustedes
young joven
your: your book su libro; (informal) tu libro; *your shoes* sus zapatos; (informal) tus zapatos
yours: is this yours? ¿es suyo esto?; (informal) ¿es tuyo esto?
youth hostel el albergue juvenil
ZIP code el código postal
zipper la cremallera, el cierre
zoo el zoo

Dictionary
Spanish *to English*

The gender of Spanish nouns listed here is indicated by the abbreviations "(m)" and "(f)," for masculine and feminine. Plural nouns are followed by the abbreviations "(m pl)" or "(f pl)." Spanish adjectives (adj) vary according to the gender and number of the word they describe; the masculine form is shown. In general, adjectives that end in -o adopt an -a ending in the feminine form, and those that end in -e usually stay the same. For the plural form, an -s is added. Some words are used only in certain areas of Latin America, indicated by the following abbreviations:

(Arg)	Argentina	(ElS)	El Salvador
(Bol)	Bolivia	(Gua)	Guatemala
(CAm)	Central America	(Mex)	Mexico
(Chi)	Chile	(Nic)	Nicaragua
(Col)	Colombia	(Per)	Peru
(Cos)	Costa Rica	(Uru)	Uraguay
(Cub)	Cuba	(Ven)	Venezuela

A

a *to*; a América *to America*; a la estación *to the station*; al médico *to the doctor*
a las tres *at: at 3 o'clock*
a propósito *deliberately*
abanico (m) *fan (handheld)*
abarrotes (m pl) *grocer*
abierto *open* (adj)
abogado/abogada (m/f) *lawyer*
abrelatas (m) *can opener*
abrigo (m) *coat*
abril *April*
abrir *to open*
abuela (f) *grandmother*
abuelo (m) *grandfather*
abuelos (m pl) *grandparents*
aburrido *boring*
acaba de llegar *it just arrived*
accidente (m) *accident*
aceite (m) *oil*; el aceite de oliva *olive oil*
aceituna (f) *olive*
acelerador (m) *accelerator*
¡acérquese! *come here!*
acondicionador (m) *conditioner* (hair)
acumulador (m) *battery* (car) (Mex)
adelantar *to pass* (car)
adiós *goodbye*
aduana (f) *customs*
aerodeslizador (m) *hovercraft*
aeropuerto (m) *airport*

afeitado (m) *shave*; afeitarse *to shave*
after-shave (m) *aftershave*
afueras (f pl) *suburbs*
agencia (f) *agency*
agencia de viajes (f) *travel agency*
agenda (f) *planner*
agitar *to wave*
agosto *August*
agradable *pleasant*
agradecer *to thank*
agua (m) *water*; el agua con gas *sparkling water*; el agua mineral *mineral water*; el agua potable *drinking water*; el agua sin gas *still water*
aguja (f) *needle*
agujetas (f pl) *shoelaces* (Mex)
ahora *now*; ¿y ahora qué? *what next?*
aire (m) *air*
aire acondicionado (m) *air conditioning*
ají (m) *chili*
ajedrez (m) *chess*
ajo (m) *garlic*
ajustado *tight*
ala (m) *wing*
albañil (m) *handyman, builder*
albaricoque (m) *apricot*
alberca (f) *swimming pool*
albergue juvenil (m) *youth hostel*

alcachofa (f) *artichoke*
alcohol (m) *alcohol*
alemán *German*
alérgico *allergic*
alfiler (m) *pin*
alfiler de gancho (m) *safety pin*
alfombra (f) *carpet, rug*
algo *something*
algodón (m) *cotton, cotton balls*
alguien *somebody*
almacén (m) *store, grocery store*
almohada (f) *pillow*
almuerzo (m) *lunch*
aló *hello* (response on phone, Ven)
alojamiento (m) *accommodation*
alquilar *to rent*
al tiro *immediately* (Chi)
alto *high, tall, loud*; ¡alto! *stop!*
amable *friendly*
amargo *bitter*
amarillo *yellow*
Amazonas (f pl) *the Amazon*
ambulancia (f) *ambulance*
América del norte *North America*
América del Sur *South America*
América Latina *Latin America*
americano *American*
amigo/amiga (m/f) *friend*; amigo/amiga por correspondencia (m/f) *pen pal*

amor (m) *love*
ampliación (f) *enlargement*
ampolla (f) *blister*
análisis de sangre (m) *blood test*
ananás (m) *pineapple* (Arg)
ancho *wide*; de tres metros de ancho *three meters wide*
andén (m) *platform*
Andes: los Andes *Andes*
anfiteatro (m) *lecture hall*
anfitriona (f) *hostess*
anillo (m) *ring* (wedding, etc.)
animal (m) *animal*; los animales de compañía/los animales domésticos *pets*
año (m) *year*
anteojos (m pl) *glasses* (for sight)
antes de ... *before ...*
anticonceptivo (m) *contraceptive*
anticuario (m) *antique shop*
antiséptico (m) *antiseptic*
apellido (m) *surname*
aperitivo (m) *aperitif*
apetito (m) *appetite*
aprender *to learn*
aprendiz (m) *trainee*
apretón de manos (m) *handshake*
araña (f) *spider*
árbol (m) *tree*
árbol de levas (m) *camshaft*
arcón (m) *chest* (furniture)
arena (f) *sand*
aretes (m pl) *earrings*
Argelia *Algeria*
argentino *Argentinian*
armario (m) *cupboard, wardrobe*
arreglar *to repair*
arriate (m) *flowerbed*
arriba *up*; (upward) hacia arriba
arroyo (m) *stream* (small river)
arroz (m) *rice*
arte (m) *art*
artículos de punto (m pl) *knitwear*
artista (m/f) *artist*
arvejas (f pl) *peas* (Arg, Bol, Chi, Col)
asado *roasted*
asiento (m) *seat*
asmático *asthmatic*
aspiradora (f) *vacuum cleaner*
aspirina (f) *aspirin*
atar *to tie*
aterrizar *to land*

ático (m) *attic*
atractivo *attractive*
atrasado *late*; el autobús está atrasado *the bus is late*
audífono (m) *hearing aid*
auriculares (m pl) *headphones*
Australia *Australia*
australiano *Australian*
auto (m) *car*
autobús (m) *bus* (local); el autobús del aeropuerto *airport bus*
autocaravana (f) *camper van*
automático *automatic*
automóvil (m) *car*
autónomo *self-employed*
autopista (f) *expressway, highway*
avergonzante *embarrassing*
aves (f pl) *poultry*
avión (m) *aircraft*
avispa (f) *wasp*
ayer *yesterday*
ayuda (f) *help*
ayudar *to help*
ayuntamiento (m) *town hall*
azúcar (m) *sugar*
azul *blue*

B

bailadora (f) *dancer*
bailar *to dance*
baile (m) *dance*
bajarse *to get off* (bus, etc.), *to get out*
bajo *low, short*
balandro (m) *sailboat*
balcón (m) *balcony*
balde de la basura (m) *garbage can*
balón (m) *soccer* (ball); el balón de playa *beach ball*
baloncesto (m) *basketball*
bañador (m) *swimsuit, swimming trunks*
banco (m) *bank*
banda (f) *band* (musicians)
bandeja (f) *tray*
bandera (f) *flag*
baños (m) *restrooms, bathrooms* (in public establishment); los baños de hombres *men's room*; los baños de señoras *ladies' room*
banqueta (f) *pavement*
bar (m) *bar* (drinks)
barato *cheap, inexpensive*
barba (f) *beard*
barbacoa (f) *barbecue*

barca (f) *small boat*
barco (m) *boat, ship*
bastante *enough, quite, fairly*
basura (f) *litter, garbage*
batería (f) *battery* (car)
baúl (m) *trunk* (car) (Per)
bebé (m) *baby* (CAm)
beber *to drink*
bebida (f) *drink*
beige *beige*
bencina (f) *gasoline* (Chi)
beneficios (m pl) *profits*
berenjenas (f pl) *eggplant*
biblioteca (f) *library*
bicicleta (f) *bicycle*; la bicicleta de montaña *mountain bike*
bien *good*; te sienta bien *it suits you*
bienvenido *welcome*
bigote (m) *mustache*
billete (de banco) (m) *banknote*
billetera (f) *wallet*
bizcocho (m) *sponge cake*
blanco *white*
blando *soft*
blanquillo (m) *egg* (CAm)
bloc (m) *notepad*
bloque de oficinas (m) *office block*
blusa (f) *blouse*
boca (f) *mouth*
boda (f) *wedding*
bodega (f) *basement*; *grocery store* (Gua, Nic)
boiler (m) *boiler*
boleto (m) *ticket*
boliche (m) *grocery store* (Chi, Arg, Uru)
bolillo (m) *roll* (bread)
boliviano *Bolivian*
bolsa (f) *bag, packet* (candy, chips); la bolsa de basura *garbage bag*; la bolsa de plástico *plastic bag*
bolsillo (m) *pocket*
bolso (m) *handbag*
bombilla (f) *light bulb*
bombillo (m) *light bulb* (Col)
bonito *pretty, attractive* (object)
borde (m) *edge, border, side*
borracho *drunk*
bosque (m) *forest*
bota (f) *boot* (shoe); (m) *tin, tin can*
botas de hule (f pl) *wellington boots*
botella (f) *bottle*
botón (m) *button*

bozal (m) *muzzle*

Brasil *Brazil*

brasileño *Brazilian*

brazo (m) *arm*

brevete (m) *driver's license* (Per, Col)

bridge (m) *bridge* (cards)

británico *British*

brocha (f) *paint brush*

broche (m) *brooch*

broma (f) *joke*

bronceado *suntanned*

broncearse *suntan: to get a suntan*

bruto *stupid*

buenas noches *good evening*

buenas tardes *good afternoon*

bueno *good, good to eat, tasty*

buenos días *good morning*

bufanda (f) *scarf*

burro (m) *donkey*

buseta (f) *bus* (Col, Ecu)

buzo (m) *sweater* (Arg, Uru)

buzón (m) *mailbox*

C

caballo (m) *horse*

cabello (m) *hair*

caberé (f) *nightclub*

cabeza (f) *head*

cabina telefónica (f) *phone booth*

cable alargador (m) *extension cord*

cacahuetes, cacahuates (m pl) *peanuts*

cada *each, every*; trescientos pesos cada uno *300 pesos each*

café (m) *coffee*; el café con leche *coffee with milk*; el café instantáneo *instant coffee*; el café solo *espresso*; (adj) *brown*

cafetería (f) *café*

caimán (m) *alligator*

caja (f) *box; checkout*; la caja de bombones *box of chocolates*; la caja de cambios *gearbox*

cajero (m) *cashier*; el cajero automático *ATM*

cajetilla (f) *packet* (cigarettes)

cajuela (f) *trunk* (car) (Mex)

calambre (m) *cramp*

calcetines (m pl) *socks*

calconcillos (m pl) *underpants*

calculadora (m) *calculator*

calefacción (f) *heating*; la calefacción central *central heating*

calentador (de agua) (m) *water heater*

calidad (f) *quality*

caliente *warm*

callado *quiet* (person)

calle (f) *street, road*; la calle principal *main road*

caluroso *warm*; (weather) *hot*

cama (f) *bed*

cámara fotográfica (f) *camera*

camarones (m pl) *shrimp*

cambiar *to change* (money)

cambiarse *to change* (clothes)

caminar *to walk*

camino (m) *path*

camión (m) *truck ; bus* (Mex)

camioneta (f) *camper trailer; bus* (Gua)

camisa (f) *shirt*

camiseta (f) *vest*

camisón (m) *nightgown*

campana (f) *bell* (church)

camping (m) *campsite*

camping-gas (m) *stove fuel*

campo (m) *countryside, field*

Canadá *Canada*

canadiense *Canadian*

canal (m) *canal*; el canal de Panamá *Panama Canal*

Canarias: las (Islas) Canarias *Canaries*

canasta (f) *basket*

canción (f) *song*

candado (m) *padlock*

cangrejo (m) *crab*

cansado *tired*

cantar *to sing*

capazo (m) *crib*

capó (m) *hood* (car)

capote (m) *hood* (car)

cara (f) *face*

caramelo *sweet* (adj)

caravana (f) *trailer*

carburador (m) *carburetor*

cardenal (m) *bruise*

cargador (m) *charger*

carne (f) *meat*

carne de cerdo/chancho (f) *pork*

carne de vaca (f) *beef*

carnet de conducir (m) *driver's license*

carnicería (f) *butcher shop*

caro *expensive*

carpa (f) *tent*

carpintero (m) *carpenter*

carretera (f) *road*

carrito (m) *cart*

carro (m) *car*

carta (f) *letter* (mail); *menu*; la carta de vinos *wine list*

cartera (f) *purse, wallet, handbag*

carterista (m) *pickpocket*

cartero (m) *mail carrier*

casa (f) *house, home*; en casa *at home*

casado *married*

cascada (f) *waterfall*

casi *almost*

cassette (f) *cassette*

castaño *brown* (hair)

castillo (m) *castle*

catedral (f) *cathedral*

catire *blond(e)* (Cub, Ven, Col)

católico *Catholic* (adj)

catorce *fourteen*

cazuela (f) *bowl* (for animals)

cebolla (f) *onion*

ceja (f) *eyebrow*

celular (m) *cell phone*

cementerio (m) *cemetery*

cena (f) *dinner, supper, dinner party*

cenicero (m) *ashtray*

central de autobus (f) *bus stop*

centro (m) *center*; el centro deportivo *gym*; en el centro *middle: in the middle*; centro (urbano) (m) *downtown*

cepillar el pelo *to brush* (hair)

cepillo (m) *brush* (for cleaning); el cepillo del pelo *hair brush*; el cepillo de dientes *toothbrush*

cerca (f) *fence*; (adj) *near, close*

cerdo (m) *pig*

cereza (f) *cherry*

cerilla (f) *match* (light)

cerrado *closed*

cerrar *to close*

cerro (m) *hill*

certificado (m) *certificate*

cerveza (f) *beer*

chacra (f) *farm* (small, Arg)

chaleco (m) *cardigan*

chalet (m) *villa*

chama (f) *girl* (Ven)

chamo (m) *boy* (Ven)

champiñones (m pl) *mushrooms*

champú (m) *shampoo*

chancho (m) *pig*

chapa (f) *license plate* (Arg)

charla (f) *talk*

chava (f) *girl* (Mex)

chaval (m) *boy* (CAm)

chavala (f) *girl* (CAm)

chavo (m) *boy* (Mex)

chele *blond(e)* (CAm)

cheque (m) *check*; el cheque de viajero *traveler's check*

chica (f) *girl*

chícharos (m pl) *peas*

chicle (m) *chewing gum*

chico (m) *boy*; (adj) *little, small*

chile (m) *chili* (Mex, CAm)

chileno *Chilean*

chimenea (f) *chimney, fireplace*

chocolate (m) *chocolate*

chofer (m) *driver*

cholgas (f pl) *mussels* (Chi)

chompa (f) *sweater* (Per, Bol)

chop (m) *beer* (Chi)

chubasco (m) *shower* (Mex) *(rain)*

chuleta (f) *chop* (food)

chupete (m) *lollipop*

ciclismo (m) *cycling*

ciclomotor (m) *moped*

ciego *blind* (cannot see)

cielo (m) *sky*

cien *hundred*

ciencias (f pl) *science*

cierre (m) *zipper*

cierto *true*; es cierto *it's true*

cigalas (f pl) *crayfish*

cigarrillo (m) *cigarette*

cinco *five*

cincuenta *fifty*

cine (m) *movie theater*

cinta (f) *cassette*; el cinta de vídeo *video tape*

cinturón (m) *belt*; el cinturón de seguridad *seat belt*

circulación (f) *traffic*

cita (f) *appointment*

ciudad (f) *city, town*; la Ciudad de México *Mexico City*

claro *clear* (water); *light* (adj: not dark)

clase (f) *class, lesson*

clavo (m) *nail* (metal)

claxon (m) *horn* (car)

cliente (m) *client*

cobija (f) *rug, blanket*

cobrador (m) *conductor* (bus)

cobrar *to cash*

cocer *to cook, boil* (egg, etc.); cocer al horno *to bake*

coche (m) *car*

coche-cama (m) *sleeper car*

cochecito (m) *baby carriage*

cochera (f) *garage* (for parking, Mex)

cocina (f) *stove, kitchen*

cocinero/cocinera (m/f) *cook*

coctel (m) *cocktail party*

código *code*; el código de la circulación *highway code*; el código postal *ZIP code*

codo (m) *elbow*

cofre (m) *hood*

cojín (m) *cushion*

cola (f) *line*

colada (f) *laundry* (washed)

colcha (f) *bedspread*

colchón (m) *mattress*

colchoneta (f) *air mattress*

colección (f) *collection* (stamps, etc.)

coliflor (f) *cauliflower*

collar (m) *collar* (of animal); *necklace*

colombiano *Colombian*

color (m) *color*

combinación (f) *slip* (underwear)

comedor (m) *dining room*

comer *to eat*

comida (f) *food, meal; lunch*

comisaría (f) *police station*

como *like*; como éste *like this one*

¿cómo? *how?*; ¿cómo se llama usted? *what's your name?*¿cómo dice? *pardon?, what did you say?*

cómoda (f) *chest of drawers*

compañía aérea (f) *airline*

compartimento (m) *compartment*

completamente *completely*

complicado *complicated*

compra (f) *shopping*

comprar *to buy*

compresas (f pl) *sanitary napkins*

comprometido *engaged* (to be married)

computadora (f) *computer*

con *with*

coñac (m) *brandy*

concha (f) *shell*

conchecito (m) *stroller*

concierto (m) *concert*

concurrido *crowded*

condón (m) *condom*

cóndor (m) *condor*

conejo (m) *rabbit*

conferencia (f) *conference*; la sala de conferencias *conference room*

congelador (m) *freezer*

congelados (m pl) *frozen foods*

conocer *to know* (person, place)

consulado (m) *consulate*

contador (m/f) *accountant*

contenedor de basura (m) *trash can*

contento *glad, happy*

contestador automático (m) *answering machine*

contra *against*

contraseña (f) *password*

contrato (m) *contract*

copa (f) *glass* (drinking)

corazón (m) *heart*

corazones (m pl) *hearts* (cards)

corbata (f) *tie*

corcho (m) *cork*

cordero (m) *lamb*

cordillera (f) *mountain range* (Chi)

cordones (de los zapatos) (m pl) *(shoe)laces*

correa (f) *leash* (for dog)

correcto *right* (correct)

correo (m) *mail*; el correo certificado *registered mail*; el correo electrónico *email*

Correos: (la oficina de) Correos (f) *post office*

correr *to run*

corrida de toros (f) *bullfight*

corriente *ordinary, usual*

cortadura (f) *cut*

cortar *to chop, to cut*

cortauñas (m) *nail clippers*

corte de pelo (m) *haircut*

cortina (f) *curtain*

corto *short*

coser *to sew*

cosméticos (m pl) *cosmetics*

costar *to cost*; ¿cuánto cuesta? *what does it cost?*

costarricense *Costa Rican*

crema (f) *cream* (lotion)

crema de zapatos (f) *shoe polish*

cremallera (f) *zipper*

creo que *I think that ...*

crucero (m) *cruise*

cuaderno (m) *notebook*

cuadrado *square* (adj)

¿cuál? *which?*

cu alquiera de ellos *either of them?*
¿cuándo? *when?*
¿cuánto cuesta? *what does it cost?; how much is it?*
¿cuánto hay de aquí a ...? *how far is it to ... ?*
¿cuántos años tiene? *how old are you?*
cuarenta *forty*
cuarto (m) *quarter, room;* (adj) *fourth*
cuarto de baño (m) *bathroom*
cuartos libres *vacancies* (rooms)
cuatro *four*
cubano *Cuban*
cubo (m) *bucket;* el cubo de la basura *dustbin*
cuchara (f) *spoon*
cuchillo (m) *knife*
cuello (m) *neck, collar*
cuenta (f) *bill*
cuerda (f) *string, rope*
cuerno (m) *horn* (animal)
cuero (m) *leather*
cuerpo (m) *body*
cueva (f) *cave*
¡cuidado! *be careful!*
cuidadoso *careful*
cumpleaños (m) *birthday*
cuna (f) *crib*
cura (m) *priest*
curita (f) *adhesive bandage*
curry (m) *curry*

D

dar *give;* dar la bienvenida *to welcome;* me da ... *can I have ...*
de *of;* de alguna manera *somehow;* de ida *single* (ticket)
de acuerdo *OK*
debajo de ... *below ... , under ...*
decir *say;* ¿qué ha dicho? *what did you say?;* ¿cómo se dice ...? *how do you say ... ?*
declaración (f) *statement*
dedo (m) *finger*
defensa (f) *bumper* (Mex)
delante de ... *in front of ...*
delgado *thin*
demasiado *too* (excessively)
démelo *give it to me*
dentadura postiza (f) *dentures, false teeth*
dentista (m/f) *dentist*
denuncia (f) *police report*

departemento (m) *department; apartment*
deporte (m) *sports*
derecho (m) *law, justice;* (adj) *right* (not left)
desayuno (m) *breakfast*
descansar *to rest*
descompostura (f) *breakdown* (car)
descompuesto *broken down*
descuento *discount*
desierto (m) *desert*
desmayarse *to faint*
desodorante (m) *deodorant*
despacho (m) *office* (room)
despegue (m) *take off*
despertador (m) *alarm clock*
después *then* (after); después de ... *after ...*
destapador (m) *bottle opener*
destornillador (m) *screwdriver*
detergente (m) *laundry detergent*
detrás de ... *behind ...*
devolver *return* (give back); *to be sick* (vomit)
dé vuelta (a la izquierda/derecha) *turn (left/right)*
día (m) *day;* el día de fiesta *public holiday*
diabético *diabetic*
diamantes (m pl) *diamonds*
diario (m) *newspaper*
diarrea (f) *diarrhea*
diccionario (m) *dictionary*
diciembre *December*
diecinueve *nineteen*
dieciocho *eighteen*
dieciséis *sixteen*
diecisiete *seventeen*
diente (m) *tooth*
diesel *diesel*
diez *ten*
diferente *different*
difícil *difficult*
dígame *hello* (on phone)
dinero (m) *money, cash;* no tengo dinero *I have no money*
dirección (f) *address*
direccional (f) *turn signal*
director/directora (m/f) *conductor* (orchestra)
disco (m) *record* (music)
disco compacto (m) *CD*
¡disculpe! *sorry!, excuse me!* (when sneezing, etc.)

diseñador/diseñadora (m/f) *designer*
disponible *available*
distinto *separate, different* (adj); ¡eso es distinto! *that's different!;* quisiera otro distinto *I'd like a different one*
distrito: el Distrito Federal *Mexico City* (Mex)
diversiones (f pl) *entertainment*
divertido; (odd) raro *funny*
doce *twelve*
documento (m) *document*
dólar (m) *dollar*
dolor (m) *ache, pain;* el dolor de cabeza *headache;* el dolor de estómago *stomachache;* el dolor de muelas *toothache*
domingo *Sunday*
Dominicana *Dominican* (adj)
¿dónde? *where?;* ¿dónde está ...? *where is ... ?*
dónut (m) *doughnut*
dormir *to sleep*
dormitorio (m) *bedroom*
dos two; los dos *both*
dulce *sweet* (adj: not sour)
dulces (m pl) *candy*
dunas (f pl) *sand dunes*
durante *during*
duro *hard* (not soft)

E

echar al correo *to mail*
echar el cerrojo *to bolt*
Ecuador *Ecuador*
ecuatoriano *Ecuadorian*
edificio (m) *building*
edredón (m) *comforter*
ejecutivo (m) *executive*
ejemplo (m) *example;* por ejemplo *for example*
ejotes (mpl) *beans*
él *he, him, the* (m); es para él *it's for him*
elástico *elastic*
electricidad (f) *electricity*
electricista (m/f) *electrician*
eléctrico *electric*
elevador (m) *elevator*
ella *she, her, the* (f); es para ella *it's for her*
ellos/ellas *they, them;* es para ellos/ellas *it's for them*
email (m) *email;* la dirección de email *email address*

embajada (f) *embassy*

embarazada *pregnant*

embotellamiento (m) *traffic jam*

emergencia (f) *emergency*

empaste (m) *filling (in tooth)*

empezar *to start*

empleado (m) *employee*

empujar *push*

en *on, at, in*; en inglés *in English*; en el hotel *in the hotel*; en su casa *at your place*

en aquel entonces *then, at that time*

encaje (m) *lace*

encantado *pleased to meet you*

encargado (m) *caretaker*

encendedor (m) *lighter*

encendido (m) *ignition*

enchufe (m) *plug (electrical)*

encima de ... *over ...*

encimera (f) *countertop*

encuentro: no me encuentro bien *I don't feel well*

enero *January*

enfermo/enferma (m/f) *nurse*

¡enhorabuena! *congratulations!*

ensalada (f) *salad*

en seguida *immediately*

entender *to understand*; I don't understand no entiendo

entiendo *I see*

entonces *then, so*

entrada (f) *entrance, ticket (theater, etc.)*

entre ... *between ...*

entrega (f) *delivery*

enviar por fax *to fax*

epiléptico *epileptic*

equipaje (m) *luggage*; el equipaje de mano *carry-on luggage*

equipo de música (m) *music system*

equivocación (f) *mistake*

equivocado *wrong*

era *it/he/she was*

era *you were (formal)*

éramos *we were*

eran *they were*

eras *you were (informal)*

eres *you are (informal)*

es *it/he/she is*

es *you are (formal)*

escalera (f) *staircase*; la escalera mecánica *escalator*; las escaleras *stairs*

escarcha (f) *frost*

escocés/escocesa (m/f) *Scottish*

Escocia *Scotland*

escuchar *hear*

escuela (f) *school*

ése/ésa *that, that one*; ese autobús *that bus*; ese hombre *that man*; esa mujer *that woman; ¿qué es eso? what's that?*

esmalte de uñas (m) *nail polish*

esos/esas *those, those ones*; esos hombres *those men*; esas mujeres *those women*

espacio (m) *room, space*

espalda (f) *back (body)*

España *Spain*

español/española (m/f) *Spanish, Spaniard*

especialidad (f) *field of study*

espejo (m) *mirror*

esperar *wait*; ¡espere! *wait!*

espinacas (f pl) *spinach*

esposa (f) *wife*

espuma de afeitar (f) *shaving foam*

esquí *ski resort*; la estación de metro *metro station*

esquina (f) *corner (of street)*

esquís (m pl) *skis*

está *it/he/she is*

está *you are (formal)*

estaba *it/he/she was; you were (formal)*

estábamos *we were*

estaban *they were*

estabas *you were (informal)*

estaca (f) *tent peg*

estación (f) *station*; la estación de autobuses *bus station*; la estación de esquí *ski resort*; la estación de metro *metro station*

estacionamiento (m) *parking lot*

estacionar *to park*; prohibido estacionar *no parking*

Estados Unidos *United States*

estamos *we are*

estampilla (m) *stamp*

están *they are*

estancia *farm (large, Arg, Uru)*

esta noche *tonight*

estaquilla (f) *tent peg*

estás *you are (informal)*

estatua (f) *statue*

este *east*; el Este *the East*

éste/ésta *this, this one*; este hombre *this man*; esta mujer *this woman; ¿qué es esto? what's this?*; éste es el señor ... *this is Mr. ...*

estómago (m) *stomach*

estos/estas *these, these ones*; estos hombres *these men*; estas mujeres *these women*; éstos son míos *these are mine*

estoy *I am*

estrecho *narrow*

estrella (f) *star*

estudiante (m/f) *student*

estufa (f) *stove, oven; heater*

etiqueta (f) *label*

evidente *clear (obvious)*

excelente *excellent*

exceso de equipaje (m) *excess baggage*

excursión (f) *excursion, tour*

excursionismo (m) *hiking*

exposición (f) *exhibition*

extintor (m) *fire extinguisher*

extranjero/extranjera (m/f) *foreigner*

extraño *unusual*

F

fácil *easy*

factor de protección (m) *protection factor (SPF)*

factura (f) *invoice*

facturación, la (mesa de) facturación *check-in desk*

falda (f) *skirt*

falta: no hace falta *there's no need*

familia (f) *family*

fanático (m) *fan (enthusiast)*

fantástico *fantastic*

farmacia (f) *pharmacy*

faros (m pl) *headlights*

fax (m) *fax*

febrero *February*

¡felicidades! *happy birthday!*

feo *ugly*

feria (f) *fair, trade fair; market (Arg, Uru)*

ferretería (f) *hardware store*

ferrocarril (m) *railroad*

ferry (m) *ferry*

fiebre (f) *temperature, fever*; la fiebre del heno *hay fever*

fiesta (f) *festival, party*

filete (m) *steak*

filtro (m) *filter*

fin (m) *end*; ¡por fin! *at last!*

final (m) *end*
finca (f) *farm* (small)
flash (m) *flash* (camera)
flauta (f) *flute*
flexo (m) *swing-arm lamp*
flojo *lazy*
flor (f) *flower*
florería (f) *florist*
foco (m) *light bulb* (Mex)
folleto (m) *brochure, leaflet*
fonda (f) *inn*
fondo (m) *bottom*
fósforo (m) *match* (light)
fotocopiadora (f) *photocopier*
foto(grafía) (f) *photograph*
fotografiar *to photograph*
fotógrafo (m) *photographer*
fotómetro (m) *light meter*
frambuesa (f) *raspberry*
francés *French*
frazada (f) *rug, blanket* (Mex, Ven, Chi, CAm)
frecuencia: con frecuencia *often*
fregadero (m) *sink; basin*
freír *to fry*
frenar *to brake*
freno (m) *brake*; el freno de emergencia *emergency brake*; el freno de mano *handbrake*
frente a *across from*; frente al hotel *across from the hotel*
fresas (f pl) *strawberries*
fresco *cool*
frío *cold* (adj); *I'm cold* tengo frío
frito *fried*
frontera (f) *border* (between countries)
fruta (f) *fruit*
fuego (m) *fire*; los fuegos artificiales *fireworks*
fuel-oil *diesel* (oil)
fuente (f) *fountain*
fuera *outside*
fuerte *strong*
fumar *to smoke*
funcionar *to function*
fusil (m) *gun* (rifle)
fútbol (m) *soccer*

G

gafas (f pl) *glasses* (for sight)
galería de arte (f) *art gallery*

Gales *Wales*
galés/galesa *Welsh*
galleta (f) *cookie*
gallina (f) *chicken*
gambas (f pl) *shrimp*
gancho (m) *peg*
ganga (f) *bargain*
garage (m) *garage* (for parking)
garantía (f) *guarantee*
garantizar *to guarantee*
garganta (f) *throat*
garzona (f) *waitress* (Arg, Uru, Chi); (m) *waiter* (Arg, Uru, Chi)
gasoil (m) *diesel* (Ven)
gasolina (f) *gasoline*
gasolinera (f) *gas station*
gas para el encendedor (m) *lighter fuel*
gato (m) *cat*
gay *gay* (homosexual)
gel (m) *gel* (hair)
gel de baño (m) *shower gel*
gemelos (m pl) *cuff links*
general: en general *usually*
gente (f) *people*
gerente (m/f) *manager*
ginebra (f) *gin*
glorieta (f) *roundabout*
gobierno (m) *government*
goma (de borrar) (f) *eraser*
gomita (f) *rubber band*
gordo *fat* (adj)
gorra (f) *cap* (hat)
gorro (m) *woollen hat*
gracias *thank you*
Gran Bretaña *Great Britain*
grande *big, large*
grapadora (f) *stapler*
grasa (f) *fat* (on meat, etc.)
gratis *free* (no charge)
grifo (m) *gas station* (Per)
gris *gray*
gritar *to shout*
grosellas negras (f pl) *black currants*
grueso *thick*
grupo (m) *party* (group)
guagua (f) *baby* (Chi, Per); *bus* (Cub)
guantes (m pl) *gloves*
guaraches (m pl) *sandals* (Mex)
guatemalteco *Guatemalan*
güero *blond(e)* (Mex)
guerra (f) *war*
guía (m/f) *guide*; la guía telefónica *phone book*; la guía turística *guide book*

guirantes (m pl) *peas* (Ven)
guisar *to cook*
guitarra (f) *guitar*
gustar *to like*: me gusta ... *I like* ...; me gusta nadar *I like swimming*

H

habitación (f) *room*; la habitación doble *double room*; el cuarto individual *single room*
hablar *to talk*; ¿habla ...? *do you speak* ...?; no hablo ... *I don't speak* ... *speak*
hacer *to do, make*; hacer footing *to jog*; hacer punto *to knit*; hacer transbordo *to change* (trains, etc.); hace sol *it's sunny*
hacha (m) *axe*
hacia abajo *down*
hacienda (f) *farm* (large)
hambre *hungry*; tengo hambre *I'm hungry*
hamburguesa (f) *hamburger*
hámster (m) *hamster*
harina (f) *flour*
hasta *until*
hasta luego *goodbye*
hay ... *there is/are* ...; ¿hay ...? *is/are there* ...?
helado (m) *ice cream*
herida (f) *injury*
hermana (f) *sister*
hermano (m) *brother*
hermoso *beautiful*
hervido *boiled*
hervidor de agua (m) *teakettle*
hervir *to boil* (of water)
hielo (m) *ice*
hierba (f) *grass*
hierro (m) *iron* (material)
hígado (m) *liver*
higo (m) *fig*
hija (f) *daughter*
hijastra (f) *stepdaughter*
hijastro (m) *stepson*
hijo (m) *son*
hincha (m) *soccer fan*
historia (f) *history*
hoguera (f) *campfire*
hoja (f) *leaf, sheet* (of paper)
hojas de afeitar (f pl) *razor blades*
hola *hello*
hombre (m) *man*
hombro (m) *shoulder*
homeopatía (f) *homeopathy*
Honduras *Honduras*
hondureño *Honduran*

hongos (m pl) *mushrooms*

honrado *honest*

hora (f) *hour*; ¿qué hora es? *what's the time?*

horario (m) *schedule*; el horario de apertura *opening times*

horno (m) *stove, oven*

horquilla (f) *garden fork*

horrible *awful, horrible*

hospital (m) *hospital*

hoy *today*

hueso (m) *bone*

huevo (m) *egg*

hule (f) *rubber* (material)

húmedo *damp, humid*

humo (m) *smoke*

I

idioma (m) *language*

iglesia (f) *church*

impermeable (m) *raincoat*

imposible *impossible*

impresora (f) *printer*

incendio (m) *fire* (blaze)

incluido *included*

indígena (m/f) *Native American*; (also adj)

indigestión (f) *indigestion*

infección (f) *infection*

información (f) *information*

informe (m) *report*

ingeniería (f) *engineering*

Inglaterra *England*

inglés/inglesa *English*

inhalador (m) *inhaler* (for asthma, etc.)

insecto (m) *insect*

insolación (f) *sunstroke*

insólito *rare* (uncommon)

insomnio (m) *insomnia*

instrumento musical (m) *musical instrument*

intentar *to try*

interesante *interesting*

internet (m) *Internet*

interpretar *to interpret*

intérprete (m/f) *interpreter*

interruptor (m) *switch*

intervención quirúrgica (f) *operation*

intoxicación alimenticia (f) *food poisoning*

invierno (m) *winter*

invitación (f) *invitation*

invitada (f) *guest*

inyección (f) *injection*

ir *to go*; ir a esquiar *to go skiing*; ir de compras *to go shopping*

Irlanda *Ireland*; Irlanda del Norte *Northern Ireland*

irlandés/irlandesa *Irish*

isla (f) *island*

izquierdo *left* (not right)

J

jabón (m) *soap*

jamón (m) *ham*

jarabe (m) *syrup*

jardín (m) *garden*

jaula (f) *cage*

jazz (m) *jazz*

jengibre (m) *ginger* (spice)

jerez (m) *sherry*

jeringa (f) *syringe*

jersey (m) *sweater*

jitomate (m) *tomato*

joven (f) *girl*; (m) *boy*; (adj) *young*

joyería (f) *jeweller's*

jueves *Thursday*

jugar *to play*

jugo (m) *juice*; el jugo de frutas *fruit juice*; el jugo de naranja *orange juice*; el jugo de jitomate *tomato juice*

juguete (m) *toy*

julio *July*

junio *June*

junto a *near*; junto a la puerta *near the door*

juntos *together*

justo *fair* (adj); no es justo *it's not fair*

K, L

kilo (m) *kilo*

kilómetro (m) *kilometer*

kiosko de periódicos (m) *newsstand*

klínex (m pl) *tissues*

la (f) *the*

laca (f) *hairspray*

lado de (f) *beside*

ladrón (m) *burglar, thief*

lagartija (f) *lizard*

lagarto (m) *lizard* (large)

lago (m) *lake*

lámpara (f) *lamp*

lamparilla de noche (f) *bedside lamp*

lamparita (f) *light bulb* (Arg)

lana (f) *wool*

langosta (f) *lobster*

lápiz (m) *pencil*

lapiz labial (m) *lipstick*

largo (m) *length*; (adj) *long*

las (f pl) *the*

lata (f) *tin can; tin*

lavandería automática (f) *laundromat*

lavavajillas (m) *dishwasher*

laxante (m) *laxative*

leche (f) *milk*; la leche limpiadora *cleansing milk* (for skin)

lechuga (f) *lettuce*

leer *to read*

lejía *bleach*

lejos *far, far away*

lengua (f) *tongue*

lente (f) *lens*; las lentes de contacto *contact lenses*; las lentes de contacto semi-rígidas *gas-permeable lenses*

lentes (m pl) *glasses* (for sight)

lentes de sol (m pl) *sunglasses*

lento *slow*

letra (f) *letter* (of alphabet)

levantarse *to get up*

libra (f) *pound* (money; weight); *free* (not engaged)

libre de impuestos *duty-free*

libro (m) *book*; el libro de frases *phrase book*

libro de cheques (m) *checkbook*

licor (m) *liqueur*

ligero *light* (not heavy)

lima (f) *lime* (fruit)

lima de uñas (f) *nailfile*

límite de velocidad (m) *speed limit*

limón (m) *lemon, lime*

limonada (f) *lemonade*

limpio *clean* (adj)

lindo *handsome*

línea (f) *line* (phone, etc.)

linterna (f) *flashlight*

lista (f) *list*

listo *clever; ready*

literatura (f) *literature*

litro (m) *liter*

llamar por teléfono *to telephone*

llanta (f) *tire, inner tube*

llave (f) *faucet; key*; la llave de las tuercas *tire iron*; la llave inglesa *wrench*

llegar *to arrive*

lleno (de gente) *crowded, full*; estoy lleno *I'm full*

llorar *to cry* (weep)

lluvia (f) *rain*

lo antes posible *as soon as possible*

loción *lotion* (f); la loción anti-mosquitos *insect repellent lotion*; la loción bronceadora *suntan lotion*

loco *crazy*

locoto (m) *chili* (Bol, Per)

lodo (m) *mud*

lo/la *it*

lo llevaron *it's been stolen*

lona impermeable (f) *groundsheet*

los (m pl) *the*

lo siento *I'm sorry*

luego *then, next*

lugar (m) *place, sight; ... the sights of ...*

luna (f) *moon*; la luna de miel *honeymoon*

lunes *Monday*

luz (f) *light*

M

madastra (f) *stepmother*

madera (f) *wood (material)*

madre (f) *mother*

maduro *ripe*

malas hierbas (f pl) *weeds*

maleta (f) *suitcase; trunk (car)*

maletero (m) *trunk (car)*

malo *bad, poor (quality)*

mamá *mum*

mañana (f) *morning; tomorrow*; por la mañana *in the morning*

mandar *to send*

mandarina (f) *tangerine*

manejar *to drive*

manga (f) *sleeve*

maní (m) *peanuts*

manilla (f) *handle (door)*

mano (f) *hand*

manta (f) *blanket, rug*

manteca (f) *butter (Arg, Uru)*

mantequilla (f) *butter*

manzana (f) *apple*

mapa (m) *map*

maquillaje (m) *make-up*

máquina de escribir (f) *typewriter*

máquina de fotos (f) *camera*

máquina podadora (f) *lawn mower*

mar (m) *sea*

marea (f) *tide*

mareado *faint, dizzy*

margarina (f) *margarine*

marido (m) *husband*

marimba (f) *xylophone (wooden)*

mariscos (m pl) *seafood, shellfish*

mármol (m) *marble*

martes *Tuesday*

martillo (m) *hammer*

marzo *March*

más *more*; más de ... *more than, over ...* ; más tarde *later*

mástil (m) *tent pole*

matrícula (f) *license plate*

mayo *May*

mecánico (m) *mechanic*

medianoche *midnight*

media pensión *half board*

medicina (f) *medicine*

médico/médica (m/f) *doctor*

medio *half*; media hora *half an hour*

mediodía (m) *noon*

medusa (f) *jellyfish*

mejillones (m pl) *mussels*

mejor *best/better*

me llamo... *my name is...*

melocotón (m) *peach*

melón (m) *melon*

menos *less*

mensajería de voz (f) *voicemail*

mercado (m) *market*

merienda (f) *snack*

mermelada (f) *jam*; la mermelada de naranja *marmalade*

mes (m) *month*

mesa (f) *table*; la mesa de escritorio *desk*

mesera (f) *waitress (Mex, CAm)*

mesero (m) *waiter (Mex, CAm)*

mesilla de noche (f) *nightstand*

metro (m) *subway*

mexicano *Mexican*

mi(s) *my*; mi libro *my book*; mis llaves *my keys*

mico (m) *monkey*

micro (m) *bus (Chi)*

microondas (m) *microwave*

miel (f) *honey*

miércoles *Wednesday*

mil *thousand*

minusválido *disabled*

minuto (m) *minute*

mío *mine*; es mío *it's mine*

mirar *to watch*

misa (f) *mass (church)*

miscelánea (f) *corner store*

mismo *same*; el mismo vestido *the same dress*; la misma gente *the same people*; otro igual, por favor *same again, please*

mochila (f) *backpack*

moda (f) *fashion*

modem (m) *modem*

mojado *wet*

moneda (f) *coin*

monedero (m) *purse*

monitor (m) *monitor*

mono (m) *monkey ; jogging suit (Ven)*

montaña (f) *mountain*

monumento (m) *monument*

morado *purple*

moras (f pl) *blackberries*

mordedura (f) *bite (dog)*

morder *to bite (dog)*

morir *to die*

mosaico (m) *mosaic*

mosca (f) *fly (insect)*

mosquito (m) *mosquito*

mostaza (f) *mustard*

motocicleta (f) *motorcycle*

motor (m) *engine (motor)*

motora (f) *motorboat*

mousse (f) *mousse (for hair)*

mover *to move (thing)*; moverse *to move oneself*; ¡no se mueva! *don't move!*

moza (f) *waitress*

mozo (m) *waiter*

muchacha (f) *cleaner*

mucho *much/many, a lot*; mucho mejor *much better*; mucho más despacio *much slower*; no muchos *not many*

muebles (m pl) *furniture*

muela (f) *back tooth*

muerto *dead*

mujer (f) *woman*

muletas (f pl) *crutches*

muñeca (f) *wrist*

muro (m) *wall (outside)*

museo (m) *museum*

música (f) *music*; la música clásica *classical music*; la música folklórica *folk music*; la música pop *pop music*

músico (m) *musician*

muy *very*

N

nací en ... *I was born in ...*

nada *nothing*; no queda nada *there's nothing left*; no sirve de nada *it's no use*

nadar *to swim*

nadie *nobody*

nafta (f) *gasoline (Arg)*

naranja (f) *orange (fruit)*

naranja *orange (color)*

nariz (f) *nose*

nata (f) *cream (dairy)*

natación (f) *swimming*

náuseas *sick*; siento náuseas *I feel sick*
navaja (f) *penknife*
navidad (f) *Christmas*
necesario *necessary*
necesito ... *I need ...*
negar *to deny*
negativo (m) *negative* (photo)
negocio (m) *business*
negro *black*
neozelandés/ neozelandesa (m/f) *New Zealander*
nevera (f) *refrigerator*
ni ... ni ... *neither ... nor ...*
nicaragüense *Nicaraguan*
niebla (f) *fog*
nieta (f) *granddaughter*
nieto (m) *grandson*
nieve (f) *snow*
niño/niña *child* (m/f); los niños *children*; no *no* (response), *not*; no hay de qué *you're welcome*; no importa *it doesn't matter*; no es/está ... *(s)he's not ...*
noche (f) *night*
nombre (m) *name*; el nombre de pila *first name*
normalmente *usually*
norte (m) *north*
Norteamérica *North America*
norteamericano *North American*
nosotros/nosotras *we, us*; es para nosotros/ nosotras *it's for us*
noticias (f pl) *news*
noventa *ninety*
novia (f) *girlfriend*
noviembre *November*
novio (m) *boyfriend*
nuestro *our*; es nuestro *it's ours*
Nueva Zelanda *New Zealand*
nueve *nine*
nuevo *new*
nuez (f) *nut* (fruit)
número (m) *number*
número personal (m) *PIN*
nunca *never*

O

o *or*; o bien ... o ... *either ... or ...*
obturador (m) *shutter* (camera)
occidente (m) *west*
océano (m) *ocean*; el Océano Pacífico *Pacific Ocean*; el Océano Atlántico (m) *Atlantic Ocean*
ochenta *eighty*
ocho *eight*
octubre *October*
oculista (m/f) *optician*
ocupado *busy, occupied*
oficina (f) *office* (place); la oficina de objetos perdidos *lost property office*; la oficina de turismo *tourist office*
oído (m) *(inner) ear*
¡oiga, por favor! *excuse me!* (to get attention); *waiter/waitress!*
ojo (m) *eye*
ojotas (f pl) *sandals* (Bol, Per, Ecu)
okey *OK*
ola (f) *wave*
oler *to smell*
oliva (f) *olive*
olivo (m) *olive tree*
olla (f) *saucepan*
olor (m) *smell*
oloroso *sweet* (sherry)
olvidar *to forget*
once *eleven*
ondulado *wavy* (hair)
operación (f) *operation*
operadora (f) *operator*
oporto (m) *port* (drink)
orden del día (m) *agenda*
oreja *ear* (f)
oriente *east*
oro (m) *gold*
orquesta (f) *orchestra*
oscuro *dark*; azul oscuro *dark blue*
ostra (f) *oyster*
otoño (m) *autumn*
otra vez *again*
otro *other, another*; el otro *the other one*; otra cosa *something else*; otra persona *someone else*; en otra parte *somewhere else*

P

padastro (m) *stepfather*
padre (m) *father*
padres (m pl) *parents*
pagar *to pay*; pagar al contado *to pay cash*
página (f) *page*
pago (m) *payment*
país (m) *country* (state)
pájaro (m) *bird*
pala (f) *spade*
palabra (f) *word*
palacio (m) *palace*
palanca de velocidades (f) *gear stick*
palangana (f) *bowl* (for food) (Arg, Uru)
paleta (f) *ice pop*
pálido *pale*
palmera (f) *palm tree*
pan (m) *bread*; el pan tostado *toast*
panadería (f) *bread shop*
pañal (m) *diaper*; los pañales desechables *disposable diapers*
Panamá *Panama*
panameño *Panamanian*
panqué (m) *large cake* (Col, Ven)
panqueques (m pl) *pancakes*
pantalla (f) *lampshade, screen*
pantalónes (m pl) *pants, trousers*; los pantalones cortos *shorts*
pantimedias (m pl) *pantyhose, stockings*
pantis (m pl) *pantyhose*
pants (m pl) *jogging suit* (Mex)
pañuelo (m) *headscarf*
papa (f) *potato*; las papas fritas *french fries*
papá *dad*
papel (m) *paper*; el papel de envolver/ regalo *wrapping paper*; el papel de escribir *writing paper*; el papel higiénico *toilet paper*; los papeles de filtro *filter papers*
paquete (m) *package, packet, parcel*
par (m) *pair*
para *for*; es para mí *it's for me*; para el viernes *by Friday*; ¿para qué? *what for?*; para una semana *for a week*
parabrisas (m) *windshield*
parachoques (m) *bumper*
parada (f) *stop*
paraguas (m) *umbrella*
parar *to stop*
pared (f) *wall* (inside)
pariente (m) *relative*
parque (m) *park*
parrilla (f) *grill*
parte de atrás (f) *back* (not front)
partido (m) *match* (sports); *party* (political)
pasador (m) *to bolt*; echar el pasador
pasaje (m) *fare, ticket*
pasajero (m) *passenger*
pasaporte (m) *passport*
pasas (f pl) *raisins*
pasatiempos (m) *hobby*

paseo (m) *excursion, walk* (stroll); ir de paseo *to go for a walk*
pasillo (m) *aisle, corridor*
paso elevado (m) *overpass*
pasta (f) *pasta*
pasta de dientes (f) *toothpaste*
pastel (m) *cake* (small)
pastelería (f) *bakery*
pastilla (f) *pill, tablet*; las pastillas para la garganta *cough drops*
pasto (m) *lawn*
patinar *to skid*
peatón (m) *pedestrian*
pecho (m) *chest* (part of body)
pedazo (m) *piece*
pedido (m) *order*
peinar *to comb*
peine (m) *comb*
película (f) *film, movie*; la película en color *color film*
peligroso *dangerous*
pelo (m) *hair*
pelota (f) *ball*
peluquería (f) *hairdresser*; la peluquería de hombres *barber*
peña (f) *nightclub*
penoso *embarrassing* (Mex)
pensar *to think*; lo pensaré *I'll think about it*
pensión completa *full board*
peor *worse, worst*
pepino (m) *cucumber*
pera (f) *pear*
percha (f) *coat hanger*
perejil (m) *parsley*
perfecto *perfect*
perfume (m) *perfume*
periódico (m) *newspaper*
perla (f) *pearl*
permanente (f) *perm*
permiso (m) *license*; con permiso *excuse me* (to get past)
permiso de conducir (m) *driver's license*
pero *but*
perro (m) *dog*
persianas (f pl) *blinds*
pesado *heavy*
pesca (f) *fishing*
pescadería (f) *fishmonger*
pescado (m) *fish*
pescar: ir a pescar *to go fishing*
petróleo (m) *diesel* (Arg)
pez (m) *fish* (animal)
piano (m) *piano*
piba (f) *girl* (Arg)
pibe (m) *boy* (Arg)

picadura (f) *bite* (insect)
picante *hot* (spicy)
picar *to bite* (insect)
picas (f pl) *spades* (cards)
picnic (m) *picnic*
pie (m) *foot*
pierna (f) *leg*
pieza (f) *play* (theater)
pila (f) *battery* (flashlight, etc.)
pileta (f) *swimming pool*
piloto (m) *pilot*
pilotos (m pl) *side lights*
pimienta (f) *pepper* (spice)
pimiento (m) *pepper* (red, green)
piña (f) *pineapple*
pinchazo (m) *puncture*
pintor (m) *decorator*
pintura (f) *paint*
pinza (f) *peg*
pinzas (f pl) *tweezers*
pipa (f) *pipe* (for smoking)
pirámide (f) *pyramid*
piscina (f) *swimming pool*; la piscina municipal *public swimming pool*
piso (m) *floor* (story)
pista (f) *runway*
pistola (f) *gun* (pistol)
piston (m) *piston*
piyama (f) *pajamas*
placa (f) *license plate*
plancha (f) *iron* (for clothes); a la plancha *grilled*
planchar *to iron*
plano (m) *plan*; (adj) *flat, level*
planta (f) *plant*
planta baja (f) *ground floor*
plástico (m) *plastic*
plata (f) *silver* (metal)
plátano (m) *banana*
plateado *silver* (color)
platicar *to talk*
platillo (m) *saucer*
plato (m) *plate*; el plato principal *main course*; los platos preparados *prepared meals*
playa (f) *beach*
plaza (f) *site, square* (in town); la plaza de toros *bullring*
plomero (m) *plumber*
pluma (f) *pen*; la pluma estilográfica *fountain pen*
pobre *poor* (not rich)
poco *a little*; poco común *unusual*; poco cocido *rare* (steak)
poder *to be able to*
policía (f) *police*; (m) *police officer*

política (f) *politics*
pollera (f) *skirt* (Arg, Bol)
pollo (m) *chicken*
polvo (m) *powder*; los polvos *make-up powder*; los polvos de talco *talcum powder*
pomada (f) *ointment*
ponchadura (f) *puncture* (Mex)
poner *to put*
poquito *a little*; sólo un poquito *just a little*
por *through, by, per*; por avión *by air mail*; por la noche *at night*; por noche *per night*; por todas partes *everywhere*; por allá *there, over there*
porcelana (f) *china(wear)*
por favor *please*
porotos (m pl) *beans* (Chi, Arg, Uru)
porque *because*
¿por qué? *why?*
portabebé (m) *car seat* (for baby)
portafolios (m) *briefcase*
portero (m) *caretaker*; *porter* (hotel)
portugués *Portuguese*
posible *possible*
postal (f) *postcard*
póster (m) *poster*
postigo (m) *shutter* (window)
postre (m) *dessert*
precio (m) *price*; el precio de entrada (m) *admission charge*
preferir *to prefer*
pregunta (f) *question*
presentarse en la facturación *to check in*
preservativo (m) *condom*
presupuesto (m) *budget, estimate*
prima (f) *cousin*
primavera (f) *spring* (season)
primer piso (m) *first floor*
primer plato (m) *starters*
primero *first*; de primera *first class*; primeros auxilios *first aid*
primo (m) *cousin*
principiante (m/f) *beginner*
principio (m) *start*
prisa: tengo prisa *I'm in a hurry*
privado *private*
problema (m) *problem*
producto (m) *product*; los productos de belleza *beauty products*; los productos

del hogar *household
products*; los productos
lácteos *dairy products*
profesión (f) *profession*
profesor/profesora
(m/f) *teacher*
profesor/profesora de
universidad (m/f)
professor (university)
profundo *deep*
programa (m) *schedule*
prohibido *prohibited*
prometida (f) *fiancée*
prometido (m) *fiancé*
propina (f) *tip (money)*
prueba (f) *test*
público *public*
pueblo (m) *small town,
village*
puedo *I can*; no puedo
I can't
¿puede ...? *can you ... ?*
puente (m) *bridge*
puerta (f) *door, gate*; la
puerta de embarque
departure gate
puerto (m) *harbor,
port*
pulga (f) *flea*
pulpería (f) *grocery
store* (Cos, ElS)
pulpo (m) *octopus*
pulsera (f) *bracelet*
punta (f) *tip (end)*
puro (m) *cigar*

Q

que *than*
¿qué? *what?*
quemadura (f) *burn*
quemadura de sol (f)
sunburn
quemar *to burn*
quena (f) *flute
(wooden, etc.)*
queque (m) *small cake*
(Chi, Per)
querer *to want, to love*
querido *dear (person)*
querosén, queroséno
(m) *kerosene*
queso (m) *cheese*
¿qué tal? *how are you?*
¿quién? *who?*
quinze *fifteen*
quirófano (m)
operating room
quizás *maybe, perhaps*

R

rábano (m) *radish*
radiador (m) *radiator*
radio (f) *radio*
rancho (m) *farm
(small, Mex)*
rápido *fast, quick*
raro *unusual*
rastrillo (m) *rake*
rasurarse *to shave*

rata (f) *rat*
ratón (m) *mouse*
raya (f) *part (hair)*
rebajas (f pl) *sale (at
reduced prices)*
rebasar *to pass
(in car)*
rebeca (f) *cardigan*
rebozo (m) *shawl*
recado (m) *message*
recámara (f) *bedroom*
recamarera (f) *chamber
maid*
recepción (f) *reception*
recepcionista (m/f)
receptionist
receta (f) *prescription*
recibo (m) *receipt*
recobrar algo *to get
something back*
recogida (f) *pickup
(postal)*
récord (m) *record
(sports, etc.)*
recuerdo (m) *souvenir*
redondo *round (circular)*
refrigerador (m)
refrigerator
refrigerio (m)
refreshments
regadera (f) *shower*
regalo (m) *gift*; el
regalo de cumpleaños
birthday present
regla (f) *ruler (for
measuring)*
regresar *to go/come back*
reír *to laugh*
rejilla de equipajes (f)
luggage rack
relajarse *relax*
religión (f) *religion*
relleno (m) *filling (in
sandwich, cake)*
reloj (m) *clock, watch*
remar *to row*
remolque (m) *trailer*
repollo (m) *cabbage*
República Dominicana
Dominican Republic
resaca (f) *hangover*
reservación (f)
reservation
reservar *to book*
resfriado (m) *cold
(illness)*; estoy
resfriado *I have a cold*
resorte (m) *spring
(mechanical)*
respirar *to breathe*
restaurante (m)
restaurant
resto (m) *rest
(remainder)*
retrasado *delayed*
reunión (f) *meeting*
revelar *develop (film)*
revista (f) *magazine*
rico *rich; tasty, nice
(to eat)*
rímel (m) *mascara*

rincón (m) *corner (of
room)*
riñón (m) *kidney*
río (m) *river*
rizos (m pl) *curls*
robar *to steal*
robo (m) *robbery*
roca (f) *rock (stone)*
rock (m) *rock (music)*
rodilla (f) *knee*
rojo *red*
ron (m) *rum*
ropa (f) *clothes*; la ropa
de cama (f) *bed linen*;
la ropa interior
underwear; la ropa
sucia *laundry (dirty)*
rosa (f) *rose*; (adj) *pink*
roto *broken*
rubí (m) *ruby (stone)*
rubio *blond (adj)*
rueda (f) *wheel*; la rueda
pinchada *flat tire*
rugby (m) *rugby*
ruidoso *noisy*
ruinas (f pl) *ruins*
rulos (m pl) *curlers*

S

sábado *Saturday*
sábana (f) *sheet
(bedding)*
saber *to know (fact)*;
no sé *I don't know*
sabor (m) *flavor*
sabroso *tasty, nice (to
eat)*
sacacorchos (m)
corkscrew
sacapuntas (m) *pencil
sharpener*
sacar *to bring out*
saco (m) *jacket*
saco de dormir (m)
sleeping bag
sal (f) *salt*
sala (f) *living room*
sala de espera (f)
waiting room
sala de pediatría (f)
children's ward
salchicha (f) *sausage*
salchichonería (f)
delicatessen
salida (f) *exit, departure*;
las salidas *departures*;
la salida de emergencia
emergency exit
salmón (m) *salmon*
salón (m) *lounge (in
hotel)*
salpullido (m) *rash*
salsa (f) *sauce*
¡salud! *cheers! (toast)*
sandalias (f pl) *sandals*
sandwich (m)
sandwich
sangre (f) *blood*
sartén (f) *frying pan*
sauna (f) *sauna*

secador (de pelo) (m)
hairdryer
seco *dry*
sed *thirsty*; tengo sed
I'm thirsty
seda (f) *silk*
segundo (m) *second*
(noun, adj); de
segunda *second class*
seguro (m) *insurance*;
(adj) *sure, safe*
seis *six*
selva (f) *jungle*; la
selva tropical
rainforest
semáforo (m) *traffic
lights*
semana (f) *week*; la
semana pasada *last
week*; la semana que
viene *next week*
seminario (m) *seminar*
semi-seco *medium-dry*
(wine)
señal (f) *deposit*
sencillo (m) *change*;
(adj) *simple*
señor *Mr., sir*; ¡señor!
waiter!
señora *Mrs., madam*
señorita *Miss*; ¡señorita!
waitress!
separado *separated*
septiembre *September*
ser *to be*
sereno (m) *night porter*
serio *serious*
seropositivo
HIV positive
servicio (m) *service,
department*; el servicio
de habitaciones *room
service*; el servicio de
radiología *x-ray
department*; el servicio
de urgencias
emergency department
servilleta (f) *napkin*
sesenta *sixty*
setenta *seventy*
seto (m) *hedge*
shorts (m pl) *shorts*
si *if, whether*
sí *yes*
Sida (m) *AIDS*
siempre *always*
sierra (f) *mountain,
mountain range*
siete *seven*
significar: ¿qué significa
esto? *what does this
mean?*
siguiente *next*
silla (f) *chair*; la silla de
ruedas *wheelchair*
silla de extensión (f)
deck chair
simpático *nice* (person)
sin *without*; sin plomo
unleaded
sinagoga (f) *synagogue*

sitio (m) *site*; el sitio
web *website*; el sitio
de taxis *taxi stand*
sobre (m) *envelope*
sobre todo *especially*
sobrina (f) *niece*
sobrino (m) *nephew*
soda (f) *soda water*
sofa (f) *sofa*
sofocante *stuffy*
sol (m) *sun*
solicitud (f) *application
form*
solo *alone*
sólo *just, only*
soltero *single*
(unmarried)
solución limpiadora (f)
soaking solution (for
contact lenses)
sombrero (m) *hat*
sombrilla (f) *sunshade*
somnífero (m) *sleeping
pill*
somos *we are*
son *they are*
sonreír *to smile*
sonrisa (f) *smile*
sopa (f) *soup*
sorbete (m) *ice cream*
(CAm)
sordo *deaf*
sostén (m) *bra*
sótano (m) *basement*
soy *I am*; soy de ... *I
come from ...*
spray (m) *spray*; el
spray antipulgas *flea
spray*
su(s) *its/hers/his/your*
(formal); ¿es suyo
esto? *is this yours?*
subirse *get in, get on*
(of train, bus, etc.)
subte (m) *subway* (Arg)
sucio *dirty*
sudadera (f) *sweatshirt*;
(m) *jogging suit*
sudar *to sweat*
sudor (m) *sweat*
suelo (m) *floor*; el suelo
aislante *groundsheet*
suelto (m) *change*
sueño (m) *sleep*
suerte (f) *luck*; ¡suerte!
good luck!
suéter (m) *sweater*
suficiente *enough*
supermercado (m)
supermarket
suplemento (m)
supplement
supositorio (m)
suppository
sur (m) *south*

T

tabaco (m) *tobacco*
tabla de windsurfing (f)
sailboard

tableta de chocolate (f)
bar of chocolate
tacón (m) *heel* (shoe)
taller (m) *garage* (for
repairs)
talón (m) *heel* (foot)
también *too* (also)
tampones (m pl)
tampons
tan *so*; tan bueno *so good*
tanto: no tanto *not so
much*; tanto ... como ...
both ... and ...
tapete (m) *rug, mat*
tapiz (m) *tapestry*
tapón (m) *cap* (bottle),
plug (sink)
taquilla (f) *box office,
ticket office*
tarde (f) *evening*; (adj)
late; it's getting late se
está haciendo tarde
tarjeta (f) *card*; la
tarjeta de banco *bank
card*; la tarjeta de
crédito *credit card*; la
tarjeta de embarque
boarding pass; la
tarjeta de vista
business card; la
tarjeta telefónica
phonecard
tarro (m) *mug*
tarta (f) *cake* (large)
taxi (m) *taxi*
taza (f) *cup*; *toilet*
tazón (m) *bowl* (for
food)
té (m) *tea*
techo (m) *ceiling*; *roof*
teclado (m) *keyboard*
técnico (m) *technician*
tejado (m) *roof*
tela (f) *material* (cloth)
teleférico (m) *cable car*
teléfono (m) *telephone*
televisión (f) *television*
temperatura (f)
temperature
temprano *early*
tenedor (m) *fork*
tener *have*; tengo *I
have*; no tengo *I don't
have*; ¿tiene? *do you
have?*; tengo que irme
I have to go; tengo
calor *I feel hot*; tengo
que ... *I must ...*
teñir *to bleach* (hair)
tenis (m pl) *athletic
shoes*; *tennis*
tenue *faint* (unclear)
tercero *third*
terminal (f) *terminal*
ternera (f) *veal*
terno (m) *suit* (Chi)
terraza (f) *terrace*
testigo (m) *witness*
tía (f) *aunt*
tianguis (m) *market*
(Mex)

tiempo (m) *time, weather*

tienda (f) *store, shop*; la tienda de discos *record store*; tienda de departamentos (f) *department store*

tienda (f) *tent*

¿tiene ...? *do you have ...?*

tierno (m) *baby* (CAm)

tierra (f) *land, soil*

tijeras (f pl) *scissors*

timbre (m) *bell* (door)

timbres (m pl) *stamps* (Mex)

tina (f) *bath* (tub)

tinta (f) *ink*

tinto *red* (wine)

tintorería (f) *dry cleaner*

tío (m) *uncle*

tipo de cambio (m) *exchange rate*

tirantes (m pl) *suspenders*

tirar de *to pull*

tirita (f) *adhesive bandage*

toalla (f) *towel*

tobillo (m) *ankle*

tocadiscos (m) *record player*

tocar *to feel* (touch)

tocino (m) *bacon*

todavía *yet*; todavía no *not yet*

todo *everything, all*; eso es todo *that's all*

todos *everyone*

todos los días *every day*

tomar *to take, catch* (bus, etc.); tomar el sol *sunbathe*; ¿quiere tomar algo? *would you like something to drink?*

torero (m) *bullfighter*

tormenta (f) *storm*

tornillo (m) *screw*

toro (m) *bull*

torre (f) *tower*

tortilla de huevos (f) *omelet*

tos (f) *cough*

toser *to cough*

trabajar *to work*

trabajo (m) *job, work*

tractor (m) *tractor*

traducir *to translate*

traductor/traductora (m/f) *translator*

traer *to fetch*

trainers (m pl) *athletic shoes*

traje (m) *suit* (clothing)

tranquilo *quiet*

trapo del polvo (m) *duster*

trasero (m) *bottom* (part of body)

tréboles (m pl) *clubs* (cards)

trece *thirteen*

treinta *thirty*

tren (m) *train*

tres *three*

triste *sad*

tú *you* (informal)

tu(s) *your* (informal); tu libro *your book*; tus zapatos *your shoes*; ¿es tuyo esto? *is this yours?*

tubería (f) *pipe* (for water)

tubo de escape (m) *exhaust*

tuerca (f) *nut* (for bolt)

tumbona (f) *deck chair*

tunco (m) *pig* (CAm)

túnel (m) *tunnel*

turismo (m) *sightseeing*

turista (m/f) *tourist*

U, V

último *last* (final)

un/una *a*

uña (f) *finger nail*

único *single* (only)

universidad (f) *university*

uno/una *one*

urgente *urgent*

usar *to use*

uso (m) *use*

usted *you* (formal)

ustedes *you* (plural)

útil *useful*

uvas (f pl) *grapes*

vacaciones (f pl) *vacation*

vacío *empty*

vacuna (f) *vaccination*

vagón (m) *car* (train); el vagón-restaurante *restaurant car*

vainilla (f) *vanilla*

valle (m) *valley*

válvula (f) *valve; vase*

vapor (m) *steam, steamer* (boat); al vapor *steamed*

vaqueros (m pl) *jeans*

varios *several*

vaso (m) *glass* (for drinking)

¡váyase! *go away!*

veces: a veces *sometimes*

vegetariano *vegetarian*

vehículo (m) *vehicle*

veinte *twenty*

vela (f) *sailing; candle*

velocidad (f) *speed*

vendaje (m) *bandage*

vender *to sell*

veneno (m) *poison*

venir *to come*

ventana (f) *window*

ventas (f pl) *sales*

ventilador (m) *fan* (ventilator)

ver *to see*; no veo *I can't see*

verano (m) *summer*

verde *green*

verdulería (f) *greengrocer*

verduras (f pl) *vegetables*

vestido (m) *dress*

veterinario (m) *vet*

vez: de vez en cuando *occasionally*

viajar *to travel*; viajar en avión *to fly* (by plane)

viaje (m) *journey*

vida (f) *life*

vídeo (m) *video* (film); el (aparato de) vídeo *video recorder*

vídeo-juegos (m pl) *computer/video games*

vidrio (m) *glass* (material)

viejo *old*

viento (m) *wind*

viernes *Friday*

vinagre (m) *vinegar*

vino (m) *wine*

violento *embarrassing* (Arg)

violín (m) *violin*

visita (m/f) *visitor*; (f) *visit*; las horas de visita *visiting hours*; la visita con guía *guided tour*

visitar *to visit*

visor de imagen (m) *viewfinder*

vista (f) *view*

vitaminas (f pl) *vitamin pills*

vivero (m) *garden center*

vodka (m) *vodka*

volar *to fly* (of plane, insect)

volcán (m) *volcano*

vos *you* (familiar) (Arg, Uru, Par)

voz (f) *voice*

vuelo (m) *flight*

W, Y, Z

web site (f) *website*

whisky (m) *whiskey*

y *and*

ya *already*

yo *I*

yogur (m) *yogurt*

zampoña (f) *panpipes*

zanahoria (f) *carrot*

zancudo (m) *mosquito* (Mex)

zapatería (f) *shoe store*

zapatilla (f) *washing machine*

zapatillas (f pl) *slippers*

zapatos (m pl) *shoes*

zona peatonal (f) *pedestrian zone*

zoo (m) *zoo*

zopilote (m) *vulture*

Acknowledgments

The publisher would like to thank the following for their help in the preparation of this book: Isa Palacios and Maria Serna for the organization of location photography in Spain; Restaurant Raymon at Mi Pueblo, Madrid; Magnet Showroom, Enfield, London; MyHotel, London; Peppermint Green Hairdressers, London; Coolhurst Tennis Club, London; Kathy Gammon; Juliette Meeus and Harry.

Language content for Dorling Kindersley by G-AND-W PUBLISHING
Managed by **Jane Wightwick**
Editing and additional input: **Lydia Goldsmith, Leila Gaafar**

Additional design assistance: **Lee Riches, Fehmi Cömert, Sally Geeve**
Additional editorial assistance: **Paul Docherty, Lynn Bresler**
Picture research: **Louise Thomas**

Picture credits

Key:
t=top; b=bottom; l=left; r=right; c=center; A=above; B=below

p2 **Alamy:** *ImageState / Pictor International;* p4/5 **Alamy RF:** *Image Source tl;* **Alamy:**D Hurst bl; Indiapicture bcl; p10/11 **Alamy RF:** *BananaStock cr;* **Getty:** *Taxi / James Day cBl;* **Ingram Image Library:** bl; p12/13 **Alamy RF:** *Dynamics Graphics Group / Creatas cBr; John Foxx cAr; RubberBall br;* **DK Images:** cl; **Ingram Image Library:** tl, cr; p14/15 **DK Images:** cr; **Ingram Image Library:** cl, cBl, cAr, cBr, bcr; p16/17 **Getty:** *Taxi / James Day bcr;* **Ingram Image Library:** tr; p18/19 **DK Images:** *David Murray tr;* p22/23 **DK Images:** cl, Andy Crawford cAr; Susanna Price br; Magnus Rew tcrB; **Ingram Image Library:** bcrA; p24/25 **DK Images:** clA, Dave King tcr; p28/29 **DK Images:** John Bulmer tr; Dave King cr; Matthew Ward bclA; **Ingram Image Library:** bcrA, bcr; p30/31 **Alamy RF:** *Comstock Images bcl Think Stock bclA;* **DK Images:** cl; p34/35 **Ingram Image Library:** tcr; p36/37 **DK Images:** bcl, bcr; Magnus Rew cl; **Ingram Image Library:** bl; p38/39 **Alamy RF:** *Imageshop / Zefa Visual Media cl;* **Ingram Image Library:** tcr; p40/41 **DK Images:** Peter Wilson bl; **Lee Riches:** cl; p42/43 **Alamy RF:** *Image Source tcr, cAr, cAAr;* p44/45 **Alamy:** *Jon Arnold Images br; ImageState / Ethel Davies bl; Vikki Martin cbl; Peter Titmuss bcr;* **Alamy RF:** *Iain Davidson Photographic bcll; David O'Shea bcr; Courtesy of* **Renault:** c; p46/47 **Alamy RF:** *Imageshop / Zefa Visual Media br;* **Ingram Image Library:** cr; Courtesy of **Renault:** tcrB; **Lee Riches:** bcl; p48/49 **Alamy:** *Balearic Pictures c;* **Alamy RF:** *Brand X Pictures bcl;* **DK Images:** tcr, bcl; Neil Lukas br; John Miller crA; **Lee Riches:** cl; p50/51 **Alamy:** *Peter Titmuss cr;* **Lee Riches:** cl; p52/53 **Alamy:** *Jean Dominique Dallet tcr;* **Alamy RF:** *Image Farm Inc clr; Imageshop - Zefa Visual Media tcrB;* **DK Images:** cl; p54/55 **Alamy:** *Jackson Smith cBl;* **Alamy RF:** *Brand X Pictures cl; John Foxx c; Image Source cAr; ThinkStock tcr;* **DK Images:** *Andy Crawford bcl;* p56/57 **Alamy:** *Balearic Pictures clA;* **Alamy RF:** *Brand X Pictures clAA;* **DK Images:** cl; Neil Lukas bl; John Miller tcll; **Lee Riches:** tcl; Courtesy of **Renault:** bc; p58/59 **Alamy:** *Michael Juno tcr;* **Alamy RF:** *Brand X Pictures cBl, cBBl;* **Ingram Publishing** cAAl; **DK Images:** cAl; Max Alexander cBr; p60/61 **Alamy:** *Robert Harding Picture Library bcr;* **Alamy RF:** *Image Source cAr;* **DK Images:** *Steve Gorton bl, tcrB; Pia Tryde cAAr;* **Ingram Image Library:** tcr; p62/63 **DK Images:** *Stephen Whitehorn c;* p64/65 **Alamy:** *Arcaid bcrA; Mike Kipling cl;* **Alamy RF:** *GKPhotography cBr; Goodshoot cAAr; Justin Kase tcrB;* **DK Images:** *Steve Tanner clr;* **Ingram Image Library:** tcr; p66/67 **Alamy:** *Arcaid tl;* **Alamy RF:** *Ingram Publishing cAr;* **DK Images:** tr; Stephen Whitehorn bl; **Ingram Image Library:** br; p68/69 **Alamy:** *Balearic Pictures cr; directphoto.org cAr; Doug Houghton cl; Indiapicture clB;* **Alamy RF:** *CoverSpot clB;* **Lee Riches:** cl; p72/73 **Alamy RF:** *imagebroker tcrB; Image Source cAr; Comstock Images tcr;* **Avery Weight-Tronix:** bl; p74/75 **Alamy RF:** *Doug Norman bl;* **Ingram Image Library:** c; p76/77 **Alamy:** *Balearic Pictures cBl; Indiapicture bl;* **Alamy RF:** *Coverspot clB;* p78/79 **Alamy RF:** *Luca DiCecco bcl; Steve Hamblin bcr;* p80/81 **Getty:** *Taxi / Rob Melnychuk bl;* **Ingram Image Library:** cAr; Xerox UK Ltd: tr; p82/83 **Alamy:** *wildphotos.com tcr;* **Alamy RF:** *FogStock cAAl; Momentum Creative Group cl; Shoosh / Up the Res cBl;* **Ingram Image Library:** cl; p84/85 **Alamy:** *Brand X Pictures cr; fl* **Alamy RF:** *BananaStock bcl; Comstock Images c; SuperStock tr;* **Ingram Image Library:** crB; p86/87 **Alamy RF:** *Luca DiCecco bcl;* **Getty:** *Taxi / Rob Melnychuk tc;* p90/91 **Alamy RF:** *Brand X Pictures cr;* **DK Images:** cl; David Jordan cAr; Stephen Oliver cr; **Ingram Image Library:** cBr; p92/93 **Alamy RF:** *Pixland cr;* **DK Images:** cl; Guy Ryecart tr; p94/95 **Alamy:** *David Kamm cl; Phototake Inc bcl;* **Alamy RF:** *Comstock Images cr; ImageState Royalty Free bcl;* **DK Images:** *Stephen Oliver tcr;* p96/97 **Alamy RF:** *Pixland bl;* **DK Images:** tl; **Ingram Image Library:** cr; p98/99 **Alamy:** *Andrew Linscott c;* **Shotfile** cr; **Alamy RF:** *Bildagentur Franz Waldhaeusl bl; ThinkStock br;* p100/101 **DK Images:** *Steve Gorton tcr;* p102/103 **Alamy:** *Hortus b; D Hurst bcrB;* **Alamy RF:** *image100 tcr; Barry Mason cAAr;* **Ingram Image Library:** crB; **DK Images:** *Paul Bricknell cl(6); Jane Burton bcl; Geoff Dann cl(2); Max Gibbs cl(4); Frank Greenaway cl(3); Dave King cl(1), cAr; Tracy Morgan cl(5);* p106/107 **Alamy:** *Shotfile cr;* **Alamy RF:** *Barry Mason br;* p110/111 **Alamy:** *Think Stock cr;* **DK Images:** *Andy Crawford cl;* p112/113 **Alamy RF:** *Dynamic Graphics Group / Creatas tcr; image100 tr;* **Ingram Image Library:** cl; bcrA; p114/115 **Alamy:** *John Cole cr;* **Alamy RF:** *Image Source cAr; Index Stock cAl; jackhollingsworth.com bcr;* p116/117 **Alamy RF:** *Dynamics Graphics Group / Creatas dA; John Foxx clB;* p118/119 **Alamy:** *D Hurst c;* **Alamy RF:** *Pixland tcr;* p120/121 **Alamy:** *ImageState / Pictor International cl;* **Shotfile** cBl; **Alamy RF:** *Sarkis Images tcr;* **DK Images:** bcl; p122/123 **Alamy RF:** *BananaStock cl;* **Ingram Image Library:** cr; p124/125 **Alamy:** *Image Farm Inc cl;* **DK Images:** bcl; Paul Bricknell tc(5); Geoff Dann tc(3); Max Gibbs tc(1); Frank Greenaway tc(2); Dave King tc(4); Tracy Morgan tc(6); **Ingram Image Library:** bl; p126/127 **Alamy:** *Jean Dominique Dallet clB;* **Alamy RF:** *Imageshop - Zefa Visual Media blA; Image Farm Inc bl;* p128 **DK Images.**

All other images Mike Good.